How to Live Your Life

How to Live Your Life

*Georgie
and
Julie Lewis*

Copyright © 2019 Georgie and Julie Lewis

The moral right of the author has been asserted.

Credit to Paul Burgess Photography for the cover image.

Apart from any fair dealing for the purposes of research or private study, or criticism or review, as permitted under the Copyright, Designs and Patents Act 1988, this publication may only be reproduced, stored or transmitted, in any form or by any means, with the prior permission in writing of the publishers, or in the case of reprographic reproduction in accordance with the terms of licences issued by the Copyright Licensing Agency. Enquiries concerning reproduction outside those terms should be sent to the publishers.

Please note that this book is not intended as a substitute for the medical advice of physicians. The reader should regularly consult a physician in matters relating to his/her health and particularly with respect to any symptoms that may require diagnosis or medical attention.

Matador
9 Priory Business Park,
Wistow Road, Kibworth Beauchamp,
Leicestershire LE8 0RX
Tel: 0116 279 2299
Email: books@troubador.co.uk
Web: www.troubador.co.uk/matador
Twitter: @matadorbooks

ISBN 978 1838590 208

British Library Cataloguing in Publication Data.
A catalogue record for this book is available from the British Library.

Printed and bound in the UK by T J International, Padstow, Cornwall
Typeset in 11pt Sabon MT by Troubador Publishing Ltd, Leicester, UK

Matador is an imprint of Troubador Publishing Ltd

Dinah

Thank you for your kindness, guidance, support and encouragement, all of which I have found invaluable.

I am so glad our paths crossed.

Contents

Foreword by Julie Lewis — xv
Introduction by Georgie — xx
To Clarify — xxiv

1: When People Die and Pass Back to Spirit — 1
    What happens to those who were
        very sick before returning to spirit — 7
    Where people go when they return to spirit — 8

2: How to Live a Life in Spirit — 11
    The transition from a physical state
        to a spiritual one — 11
    Life in spirit — 16
    The process that occurs before
        you return to earth — 18

The events that are needed for your return to earth	20
3: How to Make the Most of Your Life on Earth	**23**
The importance of speaking up for yourself	26
How to make the best of your life	27
How to enjoy your life on earth	29
4: How Important the Need is in Each of You to Return to Earth	**32**
The importance of embracing the opportunities offered to you	37
5: How to Spend Your Time Enjoying All This World Has to Offer	**39**
How to find what it is you think you are looking for	44
The importance of appreciating yourself	44
6: How to Care for Yourself	**49**
How to take care of your brain	54
The importance of caring for your body in regard to eating and drinking	55
The overall care of your body, re eating and drinking	56
7: The Reasons for Wishing to Incarnate on Earth	**60**
How your incarnation can help progress your world	62
How the changes in your world may affect you	65

8: How to Achieve What You Are on Earth to Achieve   68

9: How to Enjoy the Life You Live on Earth   76
    How important it is to be aware of how
    your friends reflect your positivity
    (or lack thereof)   79
    Recurring situations   81
    How important it is to take control of your life   82

10: How to Embrace All Your World Has to Offer   86
    How to enjoy your life more
    than you currently do   89
    Embracing the differences between you   93
    How to spend more time
    in the company of others   94
    Our concerns in regard to technology   95

11: How to Achieve Your Aims   97
    How to appreciate the amount of
    learning you have achieved   101
    How to achieve your aim to be
    the person you are on earth to be   103
    The importance of being able
    to embrace the fun in your life   105

12: The Learning Available from a Life in Turmoil   108
    How to respond in different ways   110
    The importance of caring for each other   115
    How to exploit opportunities presented to you   116
    The opportunities that are discarded   117
    Embracing opportunities or an easy life?   120

The importance of valuing yourself	121
Making the most of interests presented to you	124
How to spend more of your time pursuing these interests	126
How to further develop these skills	128
The need each of you seems to have regarding earning a great deal of money	129
13: Appreciation	**131**
How to cultivate as much appreciation as you possibly can	135
The importance of trying to appreciate the struggles of others	137
How to find ways to be kinder to yourself	138
How to appreciate all the wonders of your world	140
How to appreciate the opinions of others	142
Learning to speak your mind	143
How to become more aware of your own needs	145
How to recognise situations offered to you	146
14: The Importance of Feeling Grateful	**148**
How important it is to appreciate the kindness of others	152
How important it is to change the energy within your world	153
15: How to Stand Up for Yourself	**156**
The importance of speaking your mind	163

Why standing up for yourself has
such a beneficial effect on your life 166
The importance of being yourself 167
Appreciating the differences between people 170
Standing up for yourself as a step
towards reaching your potential 171
How to embrace your true self 173
How important it is to place a greater
focus on developing your skills 175
The current trend for self-acceptance 177
More on the current trend for acceptance 178

16: How to Make the Most of the Opportunities
Presented to You 180
The importance of caring for yourself 184

17: How to Make More Time for Yourself 188

18: How to Have More Fun in Your Life 192
What fun and enjoyment can offer you 193

19: Further Information About How to Make the
Most of Opportunities Offered to You 197
The importance of continuing
to develop throughout your life 200
How important it is to take up the
mantle and be as brave as you can be 201
The importance of achieving your lessons 204
How to focus your attention
on achieving your aims 207

20: How to Allow Yourself to Have a Good Life   208
    The importance of accepting
        responsibility for your own behaviour   208
    The importance of making changes to your
        life in order to accept responsibility for
        your own life and your own decisions   211
    An idea about how to take more responsibility
        for your actions   213
    The importance of learning to accept
        responsibility for your own life   215
    How is that possible?   216
    The importance of self-love   218
    How to appreciate your own importance   220

21: How to Make the Most of Your Time on Earth   223
    How important it is to remain focused   229
    How to be brave and step
        outside your comfort zone   231

22: How to Have a Clear Understanding of the
    Need to Reach Your Potential   232
    How each of you can achieve your
        potential   234
    How to begin this journey   235

23: How to Progress in This Life   237
    What is the help I am suggesting you request?   238
    Ways it may benefit you if
        you were to ask for help   240
    How to change the direction of your life   243

24: How to Make the Most of Your Skills	245
How to further develop these skills	247
How to be open with yourself	249
Why it's necessary to grasp the importance of other people in your life	251
The importance of making the most of these situations	252
How important it is to appreciate differences	252
Conclusion	254
The importance of living a spiritual life	254
How important it is to have a greater respect for the animals that share your planet	257
In conclusion	258
How to make the most of your future	261

Foreword

By Julie Lewis

Before I begin, I would like to welcome you to this book and I very much hope you find the contents enlightening. I appreciate it will be necessary for many of you to work hard to keep an open mind and I hope that is something you will be able to do. There is a great deal of information contained in these pages that many will struggle to accept, although not everything applies to everybody. However, all of what's said is delivered, via me, from spirit.

Who are spirit you might ask? They are people who are in heaven, which is, I guess, a rather more accepted description; however, they are spirit beings who reside in spirit. Most of them have had lives on earth, just like we have now, and have passed back to where we all come from. While there, many choose to remain close to loved ones on earth, others choose to offer assistance to those currently walking the earth, and the remainder do many other things.

The spirit who provided all this information is Georgie, and I will say a little about him. I say little as that's all I have. There are spirits who step forward, and almost the first thing they say is their name; however, there are many others, Georgie included, who feel their name is of no consequence. What I do know about him is that he passed during the reign of Edward VII in England, after many lives in which he achieved a great deal of learning. He was an author in life, writing books that required considerable research, although I'm told not all of them were published, and he was well respected by his peers. He was also extremely fond of his facial hair, which was rather exaggerated and fashionable at the time. I have asked for more information and he says if he gave more I'd go straight to Google to try and find out who he was… and he's right, I would. So for now that's all we get.

On returning to spirit he chose to continue with his learning and now spends his time lecturing to fellow spirits who are either new to spirit or wish to have information about how to make the best of a life on earth. In fact, each chapter is a lecture he provides to those seeking understanding. So you see, he is rather well qualified to provide this information.

You may also be asking why now, or for what purpose, and the answer to that is explained throughout the book; however, in short there are many changes occurring in our world and it is important we are as able as possible to prepare ourselves for them. Many are well under way; in some cases, however, before the healing of our world occurs there is likely to be a great deal of disharmony yet to come, so spirit feel it is important we are as prepared and informed as we can be.

There are many people around the globe who are doing their best to try and improve this world and this book is simply another of those attempts.

So, something about me: I was born in the early 1960s in South-East London, England, and I have had a lifelong interest in self-development. I have always held a belief that if I understood me better, I could make my life easier, and while it's taken many years and much unravelling I must admit life is significantly easier than it once was, and while later in the book Georgie talks of how no one is here to have an easy life, mine is definitely easier than it was. I am also continuing my self-development because I feel sure it can be even easier!

So, throughout my life I had a short career working in the personnel department of a publishing company and also the securities department of a Canadian bank before deciding I wanted to train as an osteopath. I did all my training and practised for nineteen years, retiring in early 2017. The main reason I chose to retire was so I could devote more of my time to developing my gifts.

The most obvious one is the gift of hearing what spirit are saying with sufficient efficiency to be able to produce this book. Hearing the words of spirit is something I've been aware of all my life but initially I had no understanding of where 'the voices' came from. I would generally only hear them when there was some kind of event going on in my life, and they tended to speak only a few words. There could, in fact, be years between them, which was very much the decision of my team of spirit helpers. For the most part they felt it important to keep their voices to a minimum until such time as it became appropriate to make themselves known to me.

Many of you will be aware of this yourself. Have you ever spoken and wondered where the words came from, or unexpectedly said something that really didn't sound like the type of thing you would normally say? Well, chances are that was spirit stepping forward. It needs to be said, however, that these words will only be for the benefit of you, the speaker; or the listener. They will never say anything that will have a detrimental effect on your lives as spirit live within the bounds of love and compassion. So if something is said that does not fulfil this criteria then it is not spirit. More information about this is provided in the book.

I chose to build upon this ability of mine after I visited a Mind, Body, Spirit fair and chanced to observe a channelling medium called Lindsley Cash who was demonstrating her abilities, and I knew instantly this was an avenue I wished to pursue. I am now able to converse with spirit easily. I am, however, by no means alone; there are others with this ability, but not many.

While working on this book, Georgie would visit me most mornings at around 7.30 and speak for an hour or so. I would record it and usually type it up later in the day. I would ask questions and request clarifications, which he would provide. It was very much a collaboration between us. This process took about six weeks. Any problems I had during the editing process, I only had to request Georgie and he would be there with his advice or clarifications. I want to emphasise, though, that no part of this required the taking over of my body or my voice. I was always able to stop when I wanted. It felt more like a teacher – pupil scenario really, where I would interrupt with queries when I was unclear. It was a pleasant experience as I have a very curious mind and was keen to expand my knowledge base in the ways of spirit. It is odd, though, knowing that on some level all this information is already known by us; it is simply hidden once we return to earth (again, that is explained within the book).

This now leaves me to say how much I hope you enjoy reading the contents of this book, and more than anything I hope you get a great deal from it and feel able to embrace many of the suggestions that are made. In fact, I hope it changes your life.

Introduction

By Georgie

I have written this book because I feel there is a great deal more that can be done by the people of earth than is currently being done in the hope of achieving all each of you intended to achieve when you chose to take a step forward and embrace a life on earth. I am aware that sentence may sound a little odd to those of you who are yet to appreciate the many reasons that caused you to choose to accept a life on earth, and I would like to advise you that that statement is fully elaborated upon within this book. I feel it is important more people are aware of their reasons for being on earth, as after the decision has been made to return and during the process of birth, the memories of those reasons are unfortunately removed, and as a consequence each person is unable to access their recollections of what it was that took them to earth.

Each of you had a reason, in fact each of you had many reasons for wishing to spend this time on earth, and they are all very much connected with learning and growth. I feel it is important that more of you become aware of that, and how it's possible to achieve that learning and growth. In days gone by it was possible for that learning to be obtained, as a great deal more time tended to be spent within communities or groups of people; large extended families tended to live together and work together, and this provided a great many opportunities for learning to occur. However, life on earth has progressed in recent years and it has become the trend for people to lead increasingly insular lives. People nowadays are far more dependent on technology than they are on other people, and that means they are less likely to achieve the learning they hoped for when they chose to have a life on earth. This book is very much about advising you of the types of learning each of you is there to achieve, and while it is simply not possible to go into detail about the lessons you are there to learn, it provides a great many clues about what those lessons may be and how it's possible for you to find ways to achieve that learning. I appreciate what I am saying may feel strange, but I would like to encourage you to embrace that curiosity as well as keep an open mind in the hope of improving not only the quality of your life but the amount of development you are able to achieve, as each of you is there with that sole purpose in mind.

Technology is in many ways having a detrimental effect on your lives, as it seems to be causing more of you to spend your time with technology rather than in the company of others, and this is something we would like you to be aware of and to do your best to find a way forward where it's possible to spend more of your time in the company of other people. We have no wish to remove your technology as we appreciate there are a great many benefits associated with it; however, there is a negative impact and that is how it limits the opportunities for each of you to mix with other people and subsequently learn what it was you hoped to learn during your time on earth.

I would like to point out that not everything in this book applies to everybody. Many of you are further along in your process of learning and, as a consequence, it is not necessary to take up everything that is here; however, if you feel that something applies to you, then I would like to encourage you to focus your attention on it and what is necessary to do in order to achieve greater levels of both learning and growth.

Throughout this book I tend to change between 'I' and 'we', and when I refer to 'we' it is simply we in spirit. There is a significant difference between how we operate in spirit and how you operate on earth, as in spirit we are very much more of a single mind. That is not to say we always agree on everything everybody says, but we have a much greater appreciation that everybody is entitled to their own opinion. I do not believe that such a life would benefit all of you on earth, although I think it would be highly beneficial if that were more the case as I appreciate on earth there can be extremes of behaviour which simply do not occur in spirit. It would benefit each of you on earth if there were greater levels of kindness and compassion and a desire to make the lives of your fellow man and woman somewhat easier; however, I would like to impress upon you that each of you is there for your own journey, and in many ways, it is important that that is the focus of your time while on earth. If you are able to do that with a great deal of kindness and compassion then your time on earth will be significantly enriched.

So, this leaves me to say how much I hope you are able to get a great deal from what it is I have said and explained to you, and I wish all of you well in your reading.

To clarify

This book is written with the aim of developing points throughout as I wish to avoid providing a great deal of information that can easily become overwhelming and subsequently forgotten. Instead it is my intention to provide information in smaller portions that can be built upon, which I hope proves to be a more palatable way to take on board all that I am offering you.

1
When People Die and Pass Back to Spirit

Many people in the world struggle with the thought of dying, but we would like to reassure all of you that it is a process most of you have undergone many times in the past and is something that is remarkably easy. We have been perfecting this for millennia and it is really very straightforward. Death is simply a point at which your body ceases to function; however, your soul is separate from your body and it is impossible for your soul to cease to exist. Your soul is the part of you that is spirit, and as your body ceases to function your spirit will lift from your body and rejoin us in spirit. Your return to us is always planned and there are many people who are here waiting for you.

When your time on earth has come to an end there is great joy and an opportunity to reunite yourself not only with those you have known on earth during this particular adventure, but those you have known in previous lives who are all here waiting to welcome you back home. It is a time of great pleasure and celebration. This continues for a number of days; however, it is also a time when those who have returned sometimes struggle to recall all the people who are here to celebrate their return. Gradually over the period of a few days their memories will return, and as the celebration eases it gives the returning spirit the opportunity to reflect on what they were able to achieve while on earth.

There is a process that is undergone whereby people are able to reflect on the life they led while on earth. During this period of reflection, they are able to review their life from many different angles. They observe their life from the point of view of the people they came into contact with and with whom they lived their life. This gives each of us an opportunity to become aware of how our behaviour affects others. This period of reflection can be an extremely pleasurable experience as there are many who were unaware of their kindness or how appreciated they were by others. For those people whose self-esteem was often rather low and who sometimes felt unloved it can be something of a revelation to discover how well loved they truly were and how appreciative many people felt of their presence. There are others, however, who were less than kind and may have inflicted a great deal of unpleasantness on others, and this period of reflection can be something of a wake-up call for parts of their personality that need addressing.

It is impossible for people to spend time on earth and be unpleasant to others and expect that behaviour to go unnoticed, and it is for that reason we would like to advise you there will always be repercussions on your return to spirit if the behaviour that is meted out to others is of a particularly unpleasant quality. Please be very clear about that. There are, we believe, a great many people on earth who are of the belief that it is acceptable to be unkind, brutal and of an unpleasant character, and who believe they have got away with this sort of behaviour. It is, however, never acceptable to be unpleasant to another human being. You are all on a journey with the aim of growing and learning, and it is important each of you is able to offer a level of support to others as this journey on earth is by no means easy. I will say more about that in another chapter.

This period of reflection so many of you struggle with is an opportunity to achieve what it was you failed to achieve while on earth, and that is a level of understanding and growth. All of you return to earth with the aim of achieving learning and growth, and on the occasions when a great deal of unpleasantness has been meted out to others it is an indication that the growth was unable to occur. We feel it is important everybody goes through this period of reflection in order to achieve a greater understanding of their time on earth.

A great deal of planning is required for people to return to earth to achieve what they intend to achieve, and so it is important each of you spends a period of time reflecting on how well (or not) that process was completed. It largely depends on a person's journey on earth as to how long the process of reflection will take. It may last the equivalent of a few of your days; however, it may also last many of your months, and it is the hope of those who organise this process that you are rather more knowledgeable and understanding at the end of it. That is not always the case, however, and it may be that many of you will decide in the future to return to earth in order to achieve what was not achieved on this particular journey.

Once the process of reflection has occurred it is time to return to spirit and resume the activities that many of us spend a great deal of our time pursuing, which for the most part means socialising and enjoying ourselves with many of the people we have met over the years. To be in spirit is an extremely pleasant experience and there is a great deal of socialising and entertainment that goes on. There are many people, for instance, who have a keen interest in music, and on their return to spirit they are able to pursue this love and produce beautiful sounds, either with their voices or from the instruments they choose to play. The sounds we hear from the orchestras here are truly magnificent. It is something we are particularly proud of here in spirit as the sounds we are able to produce are much higher and indeed lower than those you are able to hear on earth, and of course we believe the sounds that are produced here are far superior to anything you are able to appreciate on earth, and this is the case for so many of the arts that occur here in spirit. We are aware of a far greater colour palette than anything you are able to observe on earth, and this gives our artists far more opportunity to produce the most magnificent works of art. Many of your artists on earth will return to spirit and spend a great deal of their time, if that is their wish, in pursuing or perfecting their techniques.

There are those of you who return to spirit with a great deal of interest in your planet and the magnificence of all that is produced by Mother Nature, and once home it is possible to have a far greater appreciation of this. The colours that surround all living things are truly magnificent, and we are also able to observe far more of the energies that inhabit your earth as there are many that most of you can only dream about. We are aware many of you were told stories as children of fairies who inhabit the earth, and these are only one of the entities who are spending their time with you; there are many others, and on return to spirit, you will be able to observe these. A great deal of pleasure is obtained by those who have an interest in the goings-on of your world.

When we talk of your world we refer to the physical world as here in spirit we are all energetic beings, and by that we mean a collection of energy. Those of you who were able to spend time learning science at school will be aware that energy cannot die, it can only change, and that is what happens when people pass back to spirit; their energy changes. Each of us here has been here since the beginning of time and we will be here until the end of time; it is simply impossible for us to cease being. It has, in fact, never occurred. So you see it is important for us that while we are here in spirit there is a great deal to enjoy as we have no wish for our days to be mundane.

I have spoken of three things that it's possible to enjoy while here in spirit, but there are as many things to enjoy here as you can possibly think of. It is your choice as to how you wish to spend your time. There are many who choose to pursue more academic or scientific developments, the choice is entirely ours, and we have the equivalent of your universities for any of you who wish to pursue any level of information. The only thing we struggle to provide for people on their return is a continuation of rather poor behaviour that a number develop while on earth. This is unacceptable here and is something that really does not occur. On a person's return to spirit their energy undergoes something of a change and many of the difficulties they lived with are lifted. Energy, on return to spirit, becomes somewhat lighter.

It is a necessary part of your time on earth that in order for you to reside in a physical body your energy needs to become somewhat heavier, and as a result for many of you your behaviour towards others can be less than beneficial. This condition is lifted on your return home, and as a consequence the need for many of you to continue in this way ceases immediately. In fact, there is often a period of disappointment and sadness that a person's behaviour on earth was the way it was; however, that too provides an opportunity for them to learn and grow. So you see there are benefits all around that can occur at any time. It is simply a matter of developing the vision and the appreciation of what can be achieved.

I would also like to say something to you all about those who have struggled a great deal in your later years. There are a number of you who have chosen to neglect your body, either throughout your life or in your later years, and this is something we would like you to alter, as without a body that is able to function well your learning and growth become somewhat harder. Each of you has been given a body in order to have an opportunity to learn and grow, and it is important more of you make exercise part of your daily lives in order to ensure your body receives the care and attention it needs. It is never too late to start giving your body this care and attention. It may be necessary to start in a small way; however, it is important that a start is made and for this to become a regular habit. We cannot stress this enough as your lives have changed considerably in recent years. We appreciate it is not essential for you to achieve a level of exercise as many of you can work and socialise while sitting, but this does not work well for your body. So please spend some of your time focusing on achieving a greater level of movement and exercise in order to improve the journey you have on earth.

Many of you on your return are filled with regrets about how you spent your time on earth, and a number of those regrets are in regard to the lack of care and attention you were able to offer your body. There are also considerable regrets in regard to the lack of love many of you showed to those around you; however, I will pursue that avenue at a later date. We hope you will be able to heed what it is we are saying in this book in the hope of improving the quality of your life. We feel that this will not only benefit mankind, but you as an individual.

What happens to those who were very sick before returning to spirit

There are many people who, on their return, are simply too frail to return to the fold straight away, and it is important for these people to attend what you would call a hospital; however, it is unlike any kind of hospital you are familiar with on earth. It is an opportunity for your soul to rejuvenate and to achieve the level of energy that is necessary for when you return to spirit, although technically when you are in one of our hospitals you are in spirit. It depends on the level of sickness a person has on earth as to how long they will remain in a spirit hospital, and on occasions this can be for many years. It is unfortunate that this is the case and we are finding as time progresses that there are greater numbers of people who need to spend significant periods of time in our hospitals, and this is totally unnecessary when all that is required is a greater level of care for your body in life. Many of you may choose to offer an excuse that it is too late as your body is already struggling, but we would like to reassure you it is never too late. Ever. Please be very clear about that.

Where people go when they return to spirit

I would like to reassure you that we are amongst you much of the time. Heaven is a place on earth and we are indeed there with you, although if we choose we can soar into the sky and beyond. It is remarkably easy for us to do if that is what we choose. We can also take ourselves to anywhere on your planet we wish at a moment's notice and be there in the next moment. We can travel a great distance in no time at all. We can, if we so wish, visit any number of other planets within this solar system or even in others, although not so many choose to do that. So you see we can be anywhere we choose, though most of us choose to spend our time with those we care about on earth. We appreciate for many that will be rather difficult to understand, so I would like to try and offer you some information about how this is possible.

Each of you when you are born goes to earth to try and learn particular things, and you are placed in an environment where it is hoped that learning will occur. However, in order for a sufficient depth of learning to occur it is important to be unaware of your aims, otherwise it would be easy for you to come and learn and then return to spirit, but the learning would be of insufficient depth. So we felt it important each of you is unaware of your reasons for returning to earth, and in order for that to be achieved we remove your memories of previous lives and the knowledge of what it is you are there for, and we do this by placing what we call a veil around your energy. Each of you has your physical body, and around your physical body is an energy field, and around the edges of your energy field is what we call a veil which is a thickened area of energy that prevents you from seeing us and from remembering so much of your previous lives or the knowledge of why you are there. There are a few of you whose veil is perhaps a little thinner than it really needs to be and as a consequence you are able to see us; however, these people are very few in number.

I would also like to advise you about the vibrations of energy, as everything, and I mean everything, vibrates at a particular frequency and it is possible for each of us to be aware of others who vibrate at a similar frequency. When we pass back to spirit the frequency at which we vibrate alters considerably, and as a consequence it becomes impossible for those on earth to view those of us in spirit. Simply because a person is unable to observe something, it is no evidence at all that said thing doesn't exist, and it is important to remember that, as energy is everywhere. It is simply that those of you on earth have yet to become aware of how much energy there truly is; however, that discovery is for the future.

I think it is important to have a clear idea of what happens when people pass back to spirit and what it is we spend our time doing. I would, however, like to emphasise a point, that many of us in spirit choose to spend most of our time with those we love on earth. Many people in spirit miss speaking with their loved ones, so they spend part, or sometimes all, of their time with those on earth. It brings them comfort to know they can be with their loved ones. Often a great deal of encouragement is offered to try and help them with the lives they have chosen on earth. They are not always successful; however, that does not stop many of them from trying extremely hard to encourage those on earth to make certain decisions or pursue certain avenues. There are a great many of us here in spirit and each of us can choose to spend our time how we wish. The feeling here is one of enjoyment, and it's possible for us all to enjoy our lives and to achieve a level of satisfaction in what it is we choose to spend our time doing.

2
How to Live a Life in Spirit

The transition from a physical state to a spiritual one

As people near the end of their lives there is a great deal of preparation that goes on within spirit in order for your soul to be received. This often occurs a number of days and sometimes weeks before a person actually dies, and during that time there are many people in spirit who are preparing for that event; it is important a great deal of preparation is undergone in order to ensure the transition goes smoothly. I am of the belief that it is extremely important for as smooth a transition as possible to occur, and so people from spirit will contact your spirit or your soul and ensure a great many conversations are had between them. It is not uncommon for those of you who are reaching the end of your life to become aware of relatives around you. In fact, there are those who believe they have angels around them, and whether spirit or angels perform this task is of no consequence; it is simply necessary that this process is undergone. For some, the operators will indeed be spirit, for others they will be angels; it depends on a person's preference throughout their life, if indeed they had any preference at all. If there was no preference then it's likely to be spirit who perform this task; however, there are many of you who have something of a leaning towards the angelic realm and in these instances it is they that will perform this task.

It is important your soul is as prepared as possible for this event, and for the most part all that needs to occur are a number of discussions to ensure your spirit is fully aware of what will happen and how to leave your body at the appropriate time. We have been practising this technique for millennia and we have developed a process that is particularly efficient, especially when you consider billions of people have gone through this scenario.

So, as the time of transition nears, a number of your relatives will gather in order to welcome your spirit back home, and at the moment of death the spirit is able to leave your body and indeed return home. It is hoped there will be a number of people you will clearly recognise when this transition occurs; however, there are occasions when it is simply not possible for recognised people to be there and in these instances a collection of others will be there who have had an association with the person who is making the transition. It is important that when this occurs much comfort and ease is offered to the transitioning spirit as we wish for this to be as easy a process as possible. For many spirits who are making this transition it can be a rather traumatic time as a number of people will have been extremely ill before their passing or involved in an accident or maybe some kind of disaster, in which case the spirit may be feeling a little traumatised, hence the importance of this transition being as easy as possible.

Once the transition has occurred many relatives and friends of the transitioning spirit will gather in order to offer reassurance to the soul that is returning to spirit. In the instances when it is simply not possible to provide a recognised figure then people from previous lives will be there to greet them; very quickly memories return to the passing spirit and they will become aware of their prior friendships and relationships with those around them. So initially there may be a level of concern on the part of the transitioning spirit, but this is in fact very short-lived as memories can return very quickly. You may be wondering about those who pass in a very sudden and traumatic accident, and we would like to advise you that there are very few people who pass without any kind of preparation. It is extremely rare for an accident to occur that has not been prepared for.

Each of you on your arrival on earth will have an exit date, and some of you may in fact have a few as there may be a number of events that are planned for your life where it may be the choice of the individual to take a step out of their life and return home; however for many, in fact the majority of people, there will be one exit date.

There are those amongst you who, nearing this time, feel somewhat differently and may put in a request for an extension, and if we are able to oblige then we will; however, this is not always possible. It may be that there are extenuating circumstances that ensure a returning spirit does indeed need to return. These can vary from skills being required in spirit to there simply being no possible way for the continuation of that particular body. So you see we do our best to try and ensure this process is as easy and as comforting as possible for the person who is transitioning from your world to ours. We have been practising this for millennia and have developed an extremely efficient and comforting way to do this. There are a few people who arrive with us in something of a hysterical state, but we are able to calm them down extremely quickly and advise them of where they are and what will happen.

So you see this process is remarkably straightforward and something we would like to encourage you not to worry about and simply accept as part of your life. I am aware that may sound a little ambiguous; however, it is simply a stage within your very long life. Each of you has indeed had an extremely long life and your period on earth is merely a small portion of that.

I would like to add that currently a number of people are joining us as a result of war, and this is something that concerns us as war has no place in your world. We hope that in the not-too-distant future many of these wars will end; however, that is for another chapter. It is easy for us to observe the goings-on in areas of war, and relatives of the individual will be prepared for their passing. So you see for people to pass in a war is really no different to passing from illness or accident. We are always prepared for you to join us.

There are those amongst you who are of the belief that there are some whose passing is less than successful, and there are occasions when this does in fact occur; however, they are extremely small in number and when this does occur a great deal of effort is expended on our part to try and ensure the spirit is able to join us as soon as possible. It may be that members of your world are required to ensure this occurs and there are a number of groups of people who are able to perform this task. The hardest part for us in those instances is to ensure the spirit is where they need to be in order for their passing to occur, and we go to great lengths to ensure that is what happens. It may take a number of attempts but we never give up; we always work to ensure this is what occurs.

I am sure many of you have heard of the importance of walking into the light when you pass, and this is indeed what happens. We are the light that people need to step towards and it is important in the cases of those whose transition is less than successful that we ensure a light is available for them to walk into. Many of these people for whatever reason have a great deal of fear about stepping into the light; however, we work to try and diminish this fear and to give them as many opportunities as possible to return home to spirit.

Many of you will have heard stories of people whom you believe to be ghosts haunting certain places and there are occasions when that may be the case; however, the vast majority of those events occur when a strong emotion or event has occurred in a particular place and the memory of that emotion is somehow held within the energy of that area. As people approach that memory they are able to perhaps observe or feel or sometimes hear the events that have previously taken place. What they experience is a memory rather than the actual spirit, as it is extremely rare for spirits to not transition successfully. Please be assured of how rare this is.

Life in spirit

I have already covered a number of subjects about how people spend their time in spirit; however, there is a great deal of organisation that occurs here. Many of us work on projects and it is our aim to ensure that people's time in spirit is as enjoyable as possible. We encourage those who return to spirit with an interest in a particular subject, as we like people to use their skills and interests where they have the desire to be placed. We like very much to make the most of the skills people have acquired, although there are instances when the topics we are working on are not comparable to anything on earth, and in those instances, it is necessary for us to find people who have a possible interest in a particular area and then train them to bring them up to the level of those who are currently working on that project. This is always done from a place of interest on the part of the participating spirit; we have no wish for anybody to do anything they have no particular desire to do, and we have a great many projects that are running here. We work tirelessly to try and ensure that each of you is able to make the most of your time on earth, and many of the projects that we run will do exactly that. I feel sure some of you believe your lives are sufficiently hard that it could not be possible for any of us in spirit to be helping you; however, I would like to assure you that you are in fact never alone and there are always a number of people working with you to try and ensure your time on earth is as beneficial to you as possible. I will cover the reasons each of you chooses to return to earth in a later chapter.

A number of the projects we are currently running are done to try and ensure particular developments are achieved while on earth. We have access to the greatest minds that have ever lived and we feel it is important they are kept up to date with developments that occur in your world. We work hard to try and ensure any progress that occurs on earth is very much for the benefit of the people who inhabit it. There are occasions, I am afraid, when the people of earth develop an item which is detrimental to themselves and others, and we do what we can to try and ensure the development of that particular project fails. We are not always successful and there have been a number of developments where we have worked extremely hard to try and ensure that success does not occur; however, that is not always what happens.

I would also like to say at this point that there is a great deal we have developed in spirit that we felt your world would benefit from, and we have found ways to implant these ideas in the thought processes of particular people on earth in order to ensure your world progresses in a more beneficial way. Many of you believe you have excellent ideas; however, often those ideas come from us and it pleases us a great deal when we are able to successfully implant those ideas into your minds. It is not always easy to do as some minds are more open than others to having thoughts implanted in them; however, we work tirelessly to ensure this is what happens.

I would also like to say something to you about how we assign people to the projects we carry out here in spirit as a great deal of thought goes into deciding who the best people will be to work on particular projects. It is important that within these projects a highly cohesive state is achieved and time spent working on them is extremely enjoyable for those who choose to pursue this area of development. So a great deal of time is spent considering how best to use an individual's knowledge and skills – if, of course, that is their wish.

People who are returning to spirit are free to choose whatever skills they wish to develop, or not as the case may be. Some have a desire to relax and enjoy a significant period of time reacquainting themselves with all those they have known in previous lives, and it is only when they have spent a considerable time enjoying themselves that they feel a need to further their skills. It is then that we consider what it is they will be best suited to do.

The process that occurs before you return to earth

I have now covered much of what happens while in spirit and how it is that each of you returns, and I would like to say something about the process that occurs for your return to earth, as a great deal of time is spent to ensure you are placed in the best possible situation to achieve what it is you wish to achieve. Here in spirit there is often a need on the part of individual spirits to progress their knowledge, and there are a number of reasons for this which I will go into in a later chapter. However, before a person decides to return to earth there are a number of things their spirit will wish to learn while they are there. There is an extremely long list of possible lessons that people are encouraged to try and learn, and a returning spirit will select whichever they feel they are ready for. They will then take these choices to those who prepare spirits in order to find them the best possible experience to ensure these lessons are learned. This requires a great deal of planning and it is often the case that people are placed within families or settings that are familiar to them, and when I say that I mean the people around them. The families themselves are often people who have worked together many times before; that is not always the case, although it is for the majority. It is important that people are able to make the most of their time on earth as many of us in spirit do not feel that this is a particularly easy period in a spirit's life. To be in a physical form brings its own problems and difficulties and so we work tirelessly to ensure your journey is as beneficial to you as possible. It may be the lessons you are choosing to learn require help from other individuals, and as a consequence we need to find people who are willing to help you with your learning. This is not always easy as in order for a person to learn a particular lesson it may be they need a level of unpleasantness to occur in their life. We need to be particularly inventive to try and ensure the lessons people wish to learn can indeed be learned from particular experiences. So you see a great deal of work is required to ensure a person is placed where they are able to learn what they planned to learn.

Finding the necessary people to help with this lesson is often an arduous task as it can be difficult for people to behave in a particular way to ensure you learn a specific lesson. It may be they are required to be particularly hard on you, but that is not something many spirits have any great wish to do to another person. In many instances it requires a great deal of love on the part of the spirit who is offering to teach the lesson as they are the only ones who are willing to give so much of their time and effort to another person. A great deal of kindness and appreciation is given to those who have done their best to teach the lesson once the person returns to spirit.

I would like to point out to you that during your life when you meet people who are consistently hard on you, that is often what is happening. The people who care about you the most are typically the ones who give you so many opportunities in which to learn.

The events that are needed for your return to earth

We have looked into the matter of where a person needs to be placed in order to achieve their aims, but now I would like to speak to you on the actual process that occurs.

There are many of you on earth who have a strong desire to have a baby, and for the most part it is a desire that was placed within you when you were born. It simply requires a number of events to occur for that desire to come to the fore. There are others, however, who were certain before they incarnated that children were not something they wished to have, and that may be something that continues throughout their life. Also, there are some people who may change their mind and decide that to have a child would be something they would like. This may be your decision, or it may be our decision that we have placed within you. With all of you who choose to have children we do our best to try and ensure that is what happens; however, it may be that part of your learning occurs in the process of not having children, and while we accept that for many of you this can be a particularly difficult time it is nonetheless something you have arranged with us to be the case. There are others who, as part of your learning, have chosen to become parents but for that path to be particularly difficult. We appreciate it can be difficult for those of you on earth to have a full understanding of what is your path on some occasions. It is our aim, however, that all of you who desire to have children have that desire met at some point in your life, unless of course it was always the plan that you would not have children and for a great deal of learning to occur in that process. We appreciate a great deal of heartache can occur at this point in some people's lives and we are sorry that so many of you struggle with this; however, it is ultimately for your own benefit and you will appreciate that on your return home to spirit.

When conception occurs a returning spirit is allotted to a particular person or situation where it's possible for them to make the most of their time on earth, and as the process unfolds they are able to step into the foetus, usually at a point between about six and nine months' gestation. They will remain there until birth, and once that occurs, their journey begins. It is important to note that every child born has a different plan for what will occur throughout their life and we work extremely hard to try and ensure every person's plan is adhered to. They need as many opportunities as possible to achieve what they planned to achieve, and we work to ensure that is the case. I will say more about that in a future chapter; however, for now I would like to add that many of you are often absorbed by the differences in your children, and I would like to explain to you that this is the reason why. Each child has their own aims for their life and it is important they are given the opportunities to achieve those aims, which is the reason the life of each child is often so different.

You may be wondering why some children are born so disabled on occasions, and we would like to suggest to you that these children may in fact be the teachers. There are occasions when these children are affording their parents or those around them opportunities to learn, and they have agreed to perform this task.

I hope that the process of transition from earth to spirit and back to earth again is clearer, and in subsequent chapters I will give you more information in regard to the learning that needs to be undergone.

3
How to Make the Most of Your Life on Earth

Firstly, I would like to speak to you about the importance of enjoying your life, and then I would like to say something in regard to the reasons each of you has for choosing to incarnate on earth. You may believe we have covered this; however, there is a great deal more I can say on that subject, but I will leave the bulk of that for another chapter.

Each of you has chosen to incarnate on earth for a number of different reasons in regard to the amount of learning and growth you desire to achieve. It is important while you are trying to obtain that to have as much fun as you possibly can, and the reason for that is because we believe life on earth is a particularly arduous way to spend your time and the only way it is possible to ease those struggles is to enjoy yourself. To do this will make you feel somewhat lighter and your life will be considerably easier as a result; we cannot encourage you enough to ensure there are plentiful amounts of fun in your life.

When people are able to have a good deal of fun their lives become easier. It ensures they are able to cope with a great deal more that life on earth throws at them; however, it is also important that part of your life is about attaining the necessary skills required to cope with a life on earth, and by this I mean one should not spend one's entire life enjoying oneself, as it is necessary that a balance is achieved. There are those amongst you who choose to spend a lifetime having fun and enjoying yourselves and this does tip the balance the wrong way. That is as erroneous to life on earth as it is for those who spend their time simply running down a list of chores. Lives on earth are not meant to be spent in one particular way; it is essential to have a considerable variety of things in your life, and while we appreciate that for some of you there may be periods when you need to focus on your chores it is important to remember when that time ends that it is necessary to have a period of fun and enjoyment.

We think it's important for each of you to understand that when we say 'fun', we are referring to anything that gives you pleasure. It is necessary for a level of understanding in regard to this and 'anything that gives you pleasure' is exactly that; however, it is important to embrace the fact that this does not mean inflicting any discomfort or pain on another person or living thing. That is of the utmost importance, as there will be repercussions on your return to spirit. It is never acceptable to inflict any amount of harm or pain upon anything or anyone that lives on earth, and I hope that is clear.

It is necessary during your life on earth to make the most of your time. Each of you is there with lessons that need to be learned; however, they are not offered to you on a constant basis and it is important to not only achieve what is necessary for a life on earth, but also to fill a portion of your time with something that pleases you, for instance, hobbies. This is what hobbies were invented for: to lighten your spirit and allow you to have a great deal of fun. This is something we spend most of our time achieving while in spirit and it is difficult for us to grasp how so many of you choose to ignore the importance of fun, although we fully appreciate life on earth is considerably different to that in spirit as there are a great many chores that need to be accomplished that we simply have no need for in spirit. For those of you who struggle to find ways to enjoy yourself we would like to encourage you to spend a little time in quiet contemplation considering how you have enjoyed yourself in the past, and to perhaps resume that activity in the hope of lightening your life. Many people found it easier to enjoy themselves when they were children, and perhaps that is a part of your life that needs to be examined in order to find things that please you; however, this is not always the case and I appreciate there are many of you who were unable to have an enjoyable childhood. It is important for you to spend some of your time in quiet contemplation considering what it is that may give you a great deal of pleasure. It may be a number of attempts are needed at various tasks before it is possible to find something that gives you pleasure, and I would like to encourage you to do exactly that.

It is important everybody spends a significant portion of their life doing things that give them pleasure. We find those who choose not to do this often become particularly miserable, their lives become something of a drudge and they struggle a great deal to get up each morning and face their life, and there is simply no need. Each of you is as entitled as any other to have fun in your life.

The importance of speaking up for yourself

Nobody is on this earth to live a life that is organised entirely by another person. Each of you is responsible for your own life, and while it is true that when there are children in the family it is necessary to offer a level of care and attention to those children, it is also important that children have a level of autonomy in their lives and are able to make decisions about how they wish to spend their time. It is unacceptable for a person to enforce their opinions about how another person should live their life. It may of course be that the reason they do that is because the one being bullied is there to learn the lesson of standing up for themselves; however, that applies to only a few.

Each of you needs to be aware that you are responsible for your own life. We would like it very much if more people were able to accept responsibility for their own behaviour as there are many amongst you who choose to behave less than well and then blame that on somebody else, and that is unacceptable; however, if you are able to stand up for yourself then it becomes difficult for others to blame you for their less-than-acceptable behaviour.

How to make the best of your life

We have covered the necessity for each of you to have a level of fun within your life, and also the importance of accepting responsibility for your own life, so I would now like to speak about how easy it is for the remainder of your life to be.

Once people have those two points in their life the rest, for the most part, falls into place. It is necessary that each of you has opportunities to learn and grow, but these tend to occur at varying intervals throughout life, whether or not you are having fun or being responsible for yourself. These events are organised by people in spirit who have taken on the responsibility of ensuring as many opportunities as possible are offered to you to learn and grow, and they will do that throughout your life until such time as these lessons have been learned. Once that is the case they will no longer be presented, so it is important to do your best to learn these lessons.

The lessons that are presented to you are typically the scenarios that many of you feel are repeated to you at times throughout your life. Often you will have a sense of repetition or awareness that this scenario has been played out many times before and that is a good indication that this is something you need to learn. I would like to suggest that when these scenarios present themselves, you might try responding in a different way than you have done previously. Each of these scenarios, in order to achieve the correct amount of learning, needs a response that is different to the previous one, as there is a specific response that is required, and to continue responding in the same way offers little or no learning. While we appreciate there is a great deal of discomfort felt by the person who is doing the learning when they choose to respond in a different way, it is nonetheless important this is embraced.

When you are fortunate enough to have offered the necessary response, that particular scenario will never present itself to you again, so you can see how important it is to offer a different response each time and to overcome the discomfort involved in responding in a way that is unfamiliar to you. I am aware that offering an unfamiliar response produces a great deal of discomfort in many of you and that there will be some around you who will be somewhat surprised at your change in behaviour; however, I would like to encourage you to push through this in the hope of learning that particular lesson. There are large numbers of people who have lived many lives trying to learn a particular lesson and for a variety of reasons have chosen to avoid the learning each time a particular scenario presents itself, so that on their return to spirit they are filled with a great deal of disappointment and upset when the purpose for their journey on earth has not been achieved. (Although in instances when it is achieved there is a great deal of celebration that goes on as there are legions of you who have spent many lives trying to learn one particular lesson. There is also much jubilation here in spirit when you are able to fully appreciate what you have achieved.)

You may be wondering at this point why it is that this learning does not occur in spirit, and the reason for that is because, as energetic beings, if life becomes uncomfortable we are able to quickly move away from any situation. However, that is not possible on earth and so while there is a possibility for learning to occur it does tend to take millennia, and it is considerably quicker for us to have a life on earth and to learn what we need to learn. It is not easy to achieve this aim and all of us in spirit are fully aware of that, and that is the reason we work hard to offer as much encouragement and help as we possibly can in the hope that learning occurs.

How to enjoy your life on earth

Each of you needs to spend a little of your time considering the things that give you pleasure and to install them in your life, and one of the reasons this is so important is because on the occasions when a lesson is introduced it ceases to become the sole focus of your life. For many, when a lesson is being learned or presented to you everything else in life seems to be forgotten as the lesson requires a great deal of focus and thought on your part, and this is unnecessary. When this occurs, too much time is being given to trying to understand what is going on with another person, e.g. why they are choosing to behave in a particular way, and there is nothing to be gained from that. It is important simply to respond in a way that is unfamiliar to you. When your life has a great deal of fun and interest within it, giving this response becomes considerably easier as the problem ceases to be the focus of your life. A well-rounded life is much easier to live than one focused solely on performing a list of chores. Do you see the point I am trying to make? It is important for you all to have a well-balanced and well-rounded life so that when something within it becomes excessively important there are other things that can provide balance so your life does not become distorted. The balance of your life may alter for a while but it is possible for it to be re-established within a short period. There is nothing to be gained from a lifetime of chores as this tends to lead a person towards a great deal of misery, and that is not why you are there.

I think it is important also to point out how necessary it is to simply make the most of all that is around you. For those whose lives are particularly busy we would like to encourage you to find a way to reduce the amount of busyness, and one of those ways would be to try and spend a portion of each day outside. It is also important that a period of each day has a level of appreciation within it, and this can be achieved by stepping outside and appreciating what your world has to offer. Mother Nature does an admirable job in caring for your planet, and a level of appreciation is a huge investment in your own life. To be filled with the wonder of your world is an excellent way to cultivate appreciation and gratefulness. The more time you are able to offer to this, the better, as over time appreciation will permeate your life and instil in you all you have to be thankful for, as in even the most mundane life there is much to appreciate. To appreciate your surroundings changes your perspective of the world; instead of life being something of a misery with a level of dissatisfaction, it is able to alter the part of you that encourages appreciation and thankfulness. Over time, with daily practice of appreciation of Mother Nature, this part of yourself is able to grow, and this too creates a greater level of pleasure within a person's life. People in your world have so much to be thankful for but so many choose to ignore that fact. It may be that you live in a built-up city where there is not so much greenery, and, in those instances, we would like you to perhaps consider all the work that has gone into building that city, or the number of hours people have invested in making your surrounding area what it is.

There is a great deal that can be appreciated and it is simply a habit that needs to be altered, away from discontent, to appreciation and gratefulness. I cannot stress this enough as you all have a great deal to be grateful for. Another point I think it is necessary to make is an appreciation that each of you is on earth to learn and grow and have a good time, as there are many amongst you who are filled with the belief that you are the only person who has opinions and needs that need to be met, and that is simply not the case; it is important for each of you to offer a level of consideration for the lives of others. Nobody on earth finds life easy and so each of you needs to accept responsibility for your own actions and to not make the lives of others any harder.

4 How Important the Need is in Each of You to Return to Earth

I am aware parts of this have already been covered; however, I think it's important more information is offered on this subject.

I will begin this chapter by speaking of the needs people have while they are in spirit that encourage them in their desire to grow. While in spirit each of you is held together within a group which forms something like an extremely large family. Within these families there are levels of development, and within each level of development people are in a position to associate with those of that level or those who are of a lower level. If anyone has a desire to connect with those on a higher level then a request needs to be sent and the person they are wishing to contact can either fulfil this request or choose to ignore it. Often people of a higher level are busy themselves and the request is ignored. We find that over a period of years this becomes somewhat frustrating for people on lower levels and so a desire is born to increase their level of growth in the hope of elevating themselves to a higher level and therefore becoming able to associate with those they wish to associate with. Growth can be achieved in spirit; however, that generally takes a great deal of time and in order to achieve that growth in a considerably shorter time people choose to return to earth and the whole process of that return begins.

I have previously offered information about what happens on people's return to earth but I would like to add a few points. It is important for people to be clear about what it is they wish to learn, and it is also important they are given as many opportunities as possible to achieve this aim, so not only are they placed in a family where it is possible for that learning to occur; they are offered a selection of guides who will help them with this aim. Everybody who incarnates on earth has with them a spiritual guide, a member of the angelic realm, and a person we call a doorkeeper or gatekeeper. These people are with them to ensure their journey is as efficient as it can possibly be. The guide and the member of the angelic realm will perform similar tasks and it depends on the preference of the individual as to whether they are more comfortable working with a spiritual or angelic being. It really is their choice, but it may be they have no preference, in which case it is usually the spiritual being who will step forward to fulfil that role. The gatekeeper on the other hand is there to offer protection and typically remains in the background. It is unusual for people on earth to become aware of the gatekeeper as they generally have a role that has little to do with the development of the individual.

There are also a number of other spirit guides who will take a minor role and they will work on a temporary basis while they are assigned to a particular individual. They are not with them constantly; they tend to come and go as their presence is required. It may be necessary for the main guide or the angelic being to acquire information in order for them to offer the best guidance to their charge, and that is the job of their spiritual assignees. They work extremely hard to try and ensure the main guides are furnished with sufficient information in order for the journeying soul to learn as much of what they planned to learn as possible, and the main guide or angelic being will offer as much guidance as they can in order to ensure this aim is met. They work tirelessly in the hope of guiding individuals in the right direction with the aim of ensuring they have as many opportunities as possible to learn and grow; however, this depends on the requests of the individuals as to what those opportunities might be.

Before incarnating on earth there are large meetings with all the necessary people to ensure that everybody is clear on exactly what needs to be done, and once everybody is clear and a suitable position is found the individual who is seeking growth is able to proceed. This takes a considerable length of time to prepare as it is not a task in which rushing has any value.

Once a person has incarnated it is the job of the beings who accompany them to ensure their needs are met, and it is very much the aim of all the guides to ensure this is what happens. There are occasions when this growth is achieved early in a person's life, in which case the remainder of their life becomes somewhat easy; however, there are others who struggle to learn or have become rather fearful of trying to respond in different ways, in which case their learning fails to occur and their lives feel like a constant struggle as they are given one opportunity after another. This makes life extremely difficult for the individual in question; however, we hope that eventually learning will occur and these challenges will diminish. If, on the other hand, a person has tried on many occasions to master a particular challenge it may be that the guides decide to increase the intensity in order for the learning to occur. It may be that a person has spent many lifetimes working to learn a particular lesson and so their guides may decide to work harder to try and ensure this lesson is learned, in which case it may be that the person is presented with a somewhat difficult challenge in the hope of achieving their learning. It is unfortunate when this becomes necessary as so many people have a desire to grow and yet while on earth lives become rather narrow as people are often beset by a great many fears, and it is these fears that limit the amount of growth a person is able to achieve. This seems to be something unique to earth life, and makes it extremely difficult to achieve what it was they intended to achieve. Their guides work tirelessly to try and break down these fears; however, it is extremely difficult as people become set in their ways and have little desire to break free from their old lives. It is unfortunate that this is the route people choose to take as there is little to be gained by remaining in a rather closed-off and inhibited state.

There are countless things on earth that are wondrous, and wonderful opportunities to experience, but for many it seems preferable to remain in a rather sheltered life and choose not to experience any of the wondrous things that are available.

We cannot describe the disappointment this gives us as each of you while in spirit is free from these fears and it is disappointing to watch you limit the development of your life due to these imagined fears. When we speak of these fears we are referring to things like the fear of putting yourself forward for something, or avoiding a particular adventure in the belief you will be judged or harm will come to you, as for the most part that is simply not the case. There is a great deal to be gained by stepping outside your comfort zone and embracing all that life has to offer, and we urge each of you to be as brave as you can be and make the most of your time on earth as there is so much for you to achieve while you are there.

While in spirit your life is indeed bounteous and fulfilling, however, it is very different to the life you will have on earth, so we urge each of you to make the most of your time on earth, explore all the places you wish to explore and form all the relationships you wish to form. There is indeed a great deal to be gained.

Each time you are able to achieve what it is you are there to achieve there is a considerable amount of celebration that goes on here in spirit as not only does your greater spiritual team have a need to celebrate, but also your friends and relatives in spirit are able to appreciate what you have achieved. There is a great deal of partying and celebration on your return home when you become aware of what you have learned. So you see, it is important for each of you to embrace the life you live on earth, step out of your comfort zone and enjoy all that life has to offer.

The importance of embracing the opportunities offered to you

As I have just said, many opportunities are wasted due to people's fears, but I would like to offer a suggestion which I hope will encourage you to embrace those fears and make the most of your time on earth.

While in spirit we have millennia to speak of our time on earth; we spend a great deal of time going over what we were able to achieve and reliving many of the adventures we had, and for those whose life was full of fear their opportunities to relate their adventures are somewhat limited. In fact many people have a level of embarrassment when talking of their lives on earth as they were rather limited in what they allowed themselves to embrace. In spirit those who speak the most highly of their times on earth are the ones who felt able to step outside their comfort zone and embrace all that life on earth had to offer; they speak tirelessly of all the adventures they were able to have, the places they were able to go and the people they were able to meet. There is a great deal to be said for that, as once all your lessons are learned there is little need to return to earth and many choose not to, as they appreciate life on earth is not a particularly easy path.

So you see there are only a limited number of opportunities in which to achieve adventures and topics of conversation for while you are in spirit. So again, I will urge all of you to make the most of your time on earth, to embrace all it has to offer and to be as brave as you possibly can in the hope of experiencing new relationships and new adventures. Be brave, children; step forward into your magnificence and become the person you hoped you would be while you are on earth. Many of you have such high hopes for what you wish to achieve and it seems that before a person reaches adulthood they are gripped by so many fears they are unable to experience half of what they hoped for before they came to earth. The sadness that brings us is truly immense, and indeed a great deal of sadness is experienced on your return home because for many it was impossible to break free of their fears. We say this very much with your best interests at heart and we work hard to try and encourage all of you to make the most of your time on earth and to experience everything that life has to offer. Be brave; embrace your world.

5
How to Spend Your Time Enjoying All This World Has to Offer

Firstly, I would like to say how important it is for you to make the most of your time on earth, to enjoy all that is available in whatever form it presents itself (provided no suffering is afforded to anyone or any living thing). Life is a magnificent opportunity and it becomes something of a disappointment and sadness for those of you who choose not to make the most of it.

I would like to offer some further information about the opportunities that are offered to you as I am aware many of you are oblivious to these. For so many there seems to be something of a distortion in what is needed to maintain life on earth; far too much time is spent focusing on the chores necessary to survive. We appreciate work is needed to some degree in order to bring financial rewards into your home to pay your living expenses; however, it is important each of you appreciates you are not there to spend your life working, and as a result your working life needs to take up only a portion of your time. It is not intended for you to work all hours, then go home and sleep and start the whole process again the next day. That is very definitely not the plan for life on earth. We appreciate a portion of your time needs to be spent earning money and a portion needs to be spent sleeping; however, a portion of your time also needs to be spent enjoying yourself and making the most of your time, and it is that portion I would like to focus on.

It is important more of you choose to increase the time you spend in the company of others in the hope of enjoying your life rather more than you currently do. Since you are there to learn and grow it is necessary for a significant portion of your time to be spent with other people in the hope you are able to have opportunities to do so. There are opportunities offered within the family and also your workplace; however, it is important to have as many chances as possible as so many of you have a long list of lessons you intend to learn. We think it is necessary to spend a good portion of your time outside work in the company of others. Not only does this give you an opportunity to learn and grow, but also ways to enjoy yourself, and we think it is important this is exploited. Many of these opportunities appear to be discarded in favour of spending more time in your workplace or performing an endless list of tasks that you believe need to be accomplished, and while we have no wish for you to be socialising every night of the week, as we appreciate a level of rest and recuperation is needed, it is important that at least some of your free time is spent enjoying yourself in the company of other people. It may be for some of you that there is a lack of available people with whom to socialise, and if this is the case then we would encourage you to spend some of your time perhaps taking classes or joining clubs where you are able to enjoy yourself. It is vital a greater focus is given to this part of your life as currently far too many of you place your focus on work and sleep, and while sleep and rest is of the utmost importance there needs to be a greater balance within your lives wherein enjoyment and socialising are given a higher priority.

We believe many people hold on to beliefs that it is important to have the appearance of being an excellent housewife, for instance, or to have a perfect home, and we would like to dispel this as really homes are there to provide shelter and protection; nothing more. They are a place for people and families to sleep, eat and enjoy each other's company. They are not intended to be the great masterpieces that so many of you hope they will be. It is simply not necessary. Your time is far better spent in the company of others, and that may be within your home or it may be outside it; it matters not, so long as there is a high level of socialising going on. Each of you needs to focus your life on the things that are important within it, and that is to ensure you are able to spend a much greater portion of your time enjoying yourself.

We are aware there are many of you who spend your lives running after your children, and this too is of a great deal of importance, and while it is necessary that your children are able to enjoy themselves, we would like to emphasise the necessity for you to enjoy yourself also. Your life is not about ensuring your children have perfect lives, it is about ensuring you *all* have magnificent lives. Your children need to be aware that your life is important also as this will provide them with an excellent idea of what being a parent is all about, and that is to have a balanced life. When children become an excessive focus within the home a distortion develops and this often progresses into adulthood with children believing their lives have a greater priority over everyone else's, and this is simply not the case. They have as much need as you to have a balanced and enjoyable life. I am aware for some of you this will come as something of a shock as many believe their children are the most important part of their life, and in some ways that is true; however, it is nonetheless vital that you are able to demonstrate to your children the importance of having fun yourself and not centring all your fun around your children.

I would now like to point out how important it is to find ways to enjoy yourself. As I have mentioned earlier many of you were able to enjoy yourselves as children rather more easily than you are now, and that is one thing for each of you to consider: whether you would like to pursue those activities as an adult. It may be you feel they have run their course and you no longer have any wish to pursue them; however, you may look back on your childhood with longing for the enjoyment you used to have, in which case we would like to encourage you to perhaps pursue some of these pastimes.

For those whose childhood was less than enjoyable we would like to suggest a period of time be spent in contemplation of what you would like to do that would give you a great deal of pleasure. It may be you need to try a number of things before you find one that suits you best, or indeed a few things that suit you.

It is crucial to give a significant amount of time to this as it lightens your life and makes it considerably easier. I have covered some of this previously; however, I think it is important it is repeated as it is of the utmost importance that a large portion of your time on earth is enjoyed. For those who spend an excessive portion of your time enjoying yourself I would like to encourage you to perhaps spend some of that time focusing on what it is that has encouraged you to lead such an unbalanced life. I appreciate that may well sound contradictory; however, balance is important. For the most part people on earth struggle to enjoy themselves and tend to lose the balance of their life that way; however, that is not always the case. There are a number who spend far too much time enjoying themselves and the balance of their life is also somewhat off. So for those of you who struggle in this way, we would like you to spend some time in quiet contemplation, in the hope of determining why enjoyment has become such a great focus in your life and perhaps what you are trying to avoid, and when you have determined that, then correct it. That may seem somewhat dismissive of your struggles; however, it is what's needed. A greater level of understanding of what you are avoiding will allow your life to progress.

How to find what it is you think you are looking for

There are a great many of you on earth who are filled with a belief that you are there to accomplish a specific task, and we would like to advise you that for many this is simply not the case. In fact, there are very few people who are there to perform a specific task, and for those that are, when the time is right we are able to ensure that task is fulfilled. It is not something you need to build your life around. For the vast majority of you it is important to simply learn, grow and enjoy yourself; there is nothing else for you to do. We hope this is clear as we are aware many struggle to take on board the reasons they are on earth and to try and understand the purpose of life. What more can you possibly achieve in life than that?

The importance of appreciating yourself

I appreciate this is a slightly different subject; however, I think it is of equal importance. When you choose to incarnate on earth each of you has a number of personalised lessons to learn, yet in every lifetime a person undertakes there are two particular lessons you always need to learn. The first is to learn to love yourself and have a high level of acceptance of yourself; the other is to learn personal responsibility, which we have covered to an extent. It is our belief that these are such important skills that each of you needs to have as many opportunities as possible to learn them in the hope that when you eventually cease returning to earth these skills are instilled in you forever.

So, how is it possible to love yourself? We appreciate this can be a difficult task to achieve, especially when one's childhood has been filled with upset or struggle, as often such children reach adulthood with the belief that they are unworthy of love, and that is simply not the case. Every person and living thing on your planet is worthy of love and appreciation, and it is important you are all aware of that.

Each of you needs to ensure there are a number of things you are able to do for yourself that reinforce the fact that you have a great deal of care and love for yourself. It may be that for some all that's needed is a little time, perhaps reading a book or soaking in the bath, but for others that is simply not enough. For some it is important that a greater appreciation is achieved for who they are. All of you need at some point in your life to be aware of how truly magnificent you are, and we mean that, as each of you truly is magnificent. In most cases the only person who is unaware of that magnificence is yourself.

We would like to encourage you to try and develop this, and there are a number of ways it can be achieved. It can be done, for instance, by spending a portion of your time doing things for yourself that please you – nobody else, only you – and by ensuring that the time you give yourself is of the highest quality. There are large numbers of you who need to speak rather more kindly to yourselves than you currently do as many are extremely brutal in this, and all it manages to do is reinforce the opinion you have of yourself and it is essential this is altered. So, we would like to encourage you, the next time a less-than-complimentary statement is made by yourself about yourself, to stop and replace that with a statement of appreciation. It may be you are currently embroiled in a situation where a person is being particularly unkind to you, and for whatever reason you choose to give yourself a hard time about this. We would like to encourage you in this instance to perhaps appreciate your own ability to weather the current storm, or perhaps to offer yourself a level of encouragement in stating how you truly feel. To spend any amount of time reinforcing what the other person is saying has no benefit to you at all. It is important to show yourself a high level of kindness. We believe if more of you were able to do this it would make speaking your truth considerably easier, as it would mean the words you are speaking are no longer coming from a place of disadvantage. It is vital each of you treasures yourself for the truly magnificent person you are.

We are aware for some of you this will take a significant length of time to achieve, and in order for that to be achieved it is essential to start the journey as soon as you possibly can – like now. Each time you catch yourself saying anything that is vaguely derogatory about yourself, stop and replace it with a statement that is appreciative of what it is you are currently going through. This may take practice but it is something we cannot encourage you enough to achieve, as we have experienced great disappointment listening to the way many of you speak to and about yourselves. It saddens us beyond belief that so many think so little of themselves that they say such harsh things to each other, and we appreciate that if more of you were kinder to yourselves the need to be so unpleasant to others would not occur. A much greater kindness offered to yourself means a much higher level of kindness is offered to others. So you see, in order for situations you find yourself in to improve it is important to lift the way you feel about yourself. No longer will people be able to speak to you in such a derogatory manner as you will no longer be in such a place where you are able to receive that information; it will pass you by.

I appreciate that may be a little difficult to understand and I will try to explain in a little more detail. If a person believes themself to be something of a victim in life then all the statements that are offered to them which are of a rather derogatory nature will be accepted; however, if that person has a great deal of love for themself and people around them speak to them in a less-than-favourable manner then they will simply be unable to take on board the statements being offered to them. It is, as you would say, like water off a duck's back. When a person has a greater level of love for themself there is also a greater level of appreciation that when a person is speaking in a less-than-kind way, they are doing that because it is *they* who are speaking from a place of turmoil or discomfort. Do you see how being able to feel better about yourself improves your ability to see the world in a rather objective manner, and to appreciate that many people who speak from a place of unkindness are doing so because they are in that place themselves? They do not do that, as so many of you believe, because it is you who is a victim; it is in fact the person meting out the unkindness that is the problem. I hope that is clear, and that from now on those of you who are less than kind in how you speak to yourselves will be able to work harder in trying to be kinder to yourselves.

I am of the belief that learning to love yourself is possibly the most important lesson you can learn, and I cannot encourage you soon enough to start learning it. For some it will take a considerable length of time, especially if you find yourself in a particularly unpleasant situation; in fact, if this is the case there is a great deal to be gained by removing yourself from that environment, if that is possible. I hope that is clear, and that many of you will begin the process of being kinder to yourselves as there is so much to be gained in your lives.

6

How to Care for Yourself

I think it is important that people have an awareness of the privilege of being provided with a healthy and able body, and the need for a great deal of care to be offered to it.

I have started a few chapters by saying I have touched on this subject before and I would like to say that again.

All of you on earth are blessed with a body which enables you to guide your way through the life you are there to lead, and I would like to ensure a greater level of care is offered to that body. There are many who choose to spend insufficient time caring for their body; yet that is the vehicle that allows you to progress on earth and I would like to offer a few suggestions regarding how to alter your current thinking and consequently take greater care of your body.

Many of you while you are young are able to take your bodies for granted as they work particularly well at this time; however, like everything else on earth they require care and attention and it is important your body receives that in order to have as many opportunities as possible to achieve what it is you are there to achieve. The most obvious way to provide the care your body needs is to ensure it receives exercise. I cannot stress that enough as there are so many of you who have chosen to ignore this, and as you age your body struggles more and more to cope. It was not so long ago that your lives were rather more active than they are now and it was not necessary for us to ensure so many of you took such great care of your bodies. There has been a complete reversal in how you live your lives as the vast majority have sedentary jobs; life expectancy has also increased, resulting in many struggling later in life, and frankly there is no need as you are all given a number of opportunities to increase your amount of movement and therefore improve the performance of your bodies. I would like it very much if you were able to offer your body some time a few times each week, if not every day, to do a significant amount of exercise. Each of you needs to be aware of just how important this is as many become infirm or frail as they age and that can significantly limit the amount of learning they are able to achieve. In later years many choose to remain in the home, or at least in some form of accommodation, and appear to accept the condition of their bodies and rarely move. I would like to inform you, however, that one of the chief regrets people have when they come back here is how little they cared for their body. Many people on arrival home express their regret that they offered so little time to this as it meant their final years were spent in a considerable amount of isolation and disappointment, and that is not something we have any wish for you to endure. For the vast majority this kind of life is entirely reversible and I am hoping the information I give will offer many more of you the opportunity to consider in greater depth how you choose to care for your body.

It is important your body is given opportunities a number of times each week where it is able to move rather more significantly than a simple walk to work and home again. It is important blood is allowed to pump around your body and your heart rate to significantly increase. It is additionally important that all parts of your body are given an opportunity to move, so it is necessary to have a good all-round exercise plan. This exercise can take many forms and really it is your choice as to how you wish to do it. It rather depends on your preferences as many of you have a desire to venture out into the countryside, and it would be an excellent way to combine this with exercise. This would have the added benefit of calming possible stress levels as spending time in nature is one of the best ways to do so.

There are a number amongst you who enjoy group sports and this is something else we would like to encourage you in as it gives a number of opportunities to meet other people. There are also those of you who are happy to attend classes in groups, often held in gymnasiums or large halls, and again we would like to encourage you to consider participating in this type of exercise. It is entirely your choice how you choose to provide exercise for your body; however, if you are struggling to decide how to do this, perhaps sit in quiet contemplation in the hope of finding a particular means of exercise that works for you.

We are aware many of you have such busy lives that it may well seem impossible to find the time for exercise, and in these instances we would urge you to be creative. If the reason for your excessive busyness is due to your family then perhaps it would be a good idea to involve the entire family in this venture, and then you will be able to instil in your children the importance of exercise. There are those amongst you whose lives are so full of work that it is difficult for you to imagine having the time to exercise; however, I cannot stress highly enough how much your life would benefit from opportunities to stretch your body and improve its overall performance. Even if all you are able to manage is an hour at lunchtime, anything is better than nothing. For those of you who are excessively busy, remember there are weekends, although I am aware there are some amongst you who choose to fill your weekends with excessive busyness as well, and we have covered that subject earlier in this book.

Having suggested a number of ways to introduce or increase the amount of exercise in your life, it is now important you actually make this a part of your life. It is all very well deciding what you will do, but it does in fact need to be done. All of you will benefit from participating in exercise, as not only does it help you feel good about yourself, it also helps to clear your mind as well as improve the health of your body. I cannot stress enough how important this is; there really are so many people who struggle a great deal in their later years and there is no need for it. If more of you had taken time to improve the performance of your bodies then this would simply not occur.

Some of you have important lessons to learn in regard to exercise and how it's important to care for yourself in this life; however, for those who do not necessarily need to learn these lessons it continues to be important to keep your body moving and to attain fitness. Each of you when you agree to return to earth is assigned a particular body and it is important that body receives your care and attention in order to achieve what you hope to achieve. There is simply no excuse for ignorance in this day and age regarding the benefits that exercise can offer to a body.

It is also important you are able to observe any possible deterioration within your body and take action when this occurs. Many people think it is better to simply ignore a part of their body that does not function quite as well as it previously did, and when they do it often means a problem that could easily be resolved becomes rather more significant, and again there is no need. Attention must be paid to your body in order to keep it as healthy as you possibly can. Some of you may find, when you do eventually decide to visit a doctor, that the condition has developed to an alarming level, and that is often an example of how little attention you are willing to offer yourself. It is important to take stock and give your body a greater degree of time and respect.

I am hopeful that upon completion of this book many of you will be inclined to spend a period of your day or week in quiet contemplation reconnecting with yourself, and that when this is done it will be possible for you to do a scan of your body to ensure it is performing as well as it can, but I will say more about that later in this book. I would, however, like to add that it is never too late to integrate a level of exercise into your life. Bodies need and appreciate movement and exercise, and as soon as these are offered your body condition will begin to improve. It may be that this needs to be done very gradually; however, it is extremely important that it is started.

Those of you who are of the belief that you have a great many problems with your body and are fearful of exercising it need to be aware that the health rewards are so vast that many of your aches and pains will in fact disappear once you begin exercising. Many struggle to take on board the importance of exercise, and so I will say this again. It is important for your body to receive a great deal of care and attention as you have been afforded an opportunity to spend a lifetime on earth with the sole aim of learning and growing, and to ignore the care of your body reduces the opportunities you have. So I hope that is clear, and that more of you will give a great deal more care and attention to your bodies from now on.

How to take care of your brain

While on earth it is imperative you are able to offer opportunities to your brain in order for it to perform its tasks. This is something many take for granted; however, your brain also needs exercise and stimulation. It is simply not enough to perform your work and return home to your family. Brains need to receive some stimulation in a way that is out of the ordinary. There are a number of ways this can be done and it is up to each of you to find a way for that to happen. This can easily be integrated into your life in a way that provides stimulation for your brain but does not encroach so much on the rest of your life, and there are many ways that this can be done. It simply requires a level of thought on your part as to the way that would suit you best. Each of you needs a level of stimulation each week that is different to the rest of your life. It may be you choose to learn something new, in which case that is all that is required; or it may be you choose to do a number of crosswords or puzzles and this too will be sufficient; in fact, these are the two main ways it is possible to stimulate your brain. This level of stimulation can easily be obtained through fun and enjoyment in whichever form you choose.

The importance of caring for your body in regard to eating and drinking

There seems to have evolved in many parts of the developed world a need to abuse your body in a number of ways. There are many people who have chosen to eat excessively and there are also a number of people who have chosen to drink alcohol excessively, and both of these excesses need to be reined in. Bodies work extremely hard and it is important that no undue strain is placed on them. It is also important each of you is able to control your need for excess.

For those who incline towards any form of excess, whether in eating or in drinking, this part of the book is for you. It is important to sit in quiet contemplation with the intention of determining the reasons you choose to eat or drink to excess. It may be that it's extremely difficult for you to process your emotions or those of other people, or that you lack the willpower to live the life you wish to live, or that there have been events in your life that you would prefer not to think about. In fact, there are a great many reasons why people choose to eat and drink to excess, and while it is all very well sitting in quiet contemplation to try and understand the reasons, it is another matter entirely to try and take on board these reasons. In this instance I would like to suggest something I think will work well for many, and that is to try and find yourself a counsellor or psychotherapist who is willing to work with you to gain a greater understanding of the reasons for this excess. For many there is an awareness of the reasons, however, up till now it has proved to be impossible to reduce the amounts that are eaten or drunk, and when I say 'drunk' I am referring to alcohol. It is necessary that a greater level of understanding is achieved regarding these reasons, and then to try and appreciate how to reduce these concerns to a level where it's possible to live a life of minimal excess. It may be important to overcome this excess as that may well be one of the lessons you are there to learn; however, if this is not dealt with early enough in your life then other problems may develop and the opportunity to participate in a full life is lost. So you see it is important that attention is given to your need to eat or drink excessively, and to do so as early in your life as possible in order to understand what it is you feel causes you to behave this way.

The overall care of your body, re eating and drinking

It is important you are able to value your body sufficiently to not only offer it exercise, but also to ensure the quality of food you are providing is sufficient. It may be you are in a position to eat a great deal and yet not increase so much in weight, and it is important this too is given attention as in time this will have a detrimental effect on your body. There are a great many foods on earth that provide much pleasure but remarkably little nourishment, and while we have no wish to remove such items from your diet entirely it is important these types of food are eaten in minute quantities. Many people choose to eat these foods on a daily basis and that, unfortunately, is not acceptable, as your body needs to receive a high level of nutrition in order to function well. If you are able to grow your own vegetables and fruits, all the better, as you will be aware of the goodness within them.

We currently have a number of concerns with the way your food industries are progressing as there is an excessive amount of pesticides being used and this in turn is having a wide-reaching effect on your planet. We are hopeful that in the not-too-distant future this will be accepted and many, if not all, pesticides will be abolished. In the meantime it is important the food you eat has as little pesticide on it as possible. If it's not possible to find organic food then please ensure your food is thoroughly washed before you eat it. We cannot stress enough the importance of minimising the intake of pesticides as this too has a long-term detrimental effect on your body. We appreciate for many this is something that will be difficult to integrate into your life, and all we can say is to try and eat as many fruit and vegetables as possible that are not sprayed with such potent pesticides.

It is unfortunate such vicious pesticides have been developed, but we are hopeful it will not be so much longer before the damage they cause is proven and for their use to cease. It is ridiculous that your foods are sprayed with so many potent chemicals and for the expectation to be that there will be no harm done, as this could not be further from the truth. A great deal of harm is being inflicted on your world with the use of pesticides; we are hopeful this development in your history will soon be reversed. All we can ask is for you to do your best to eat foods that are as naturally produced as possible without the use of pesticides, though we accept for many of you this will simply not be possible.

There is also a growing trend for many people to eat excessive amounts of sugar, and this too is something we would like to encourage you all to refrain from as there are few benefits associated with this and there is in fact a great deal of harm caused to your body. We believe also that many of you are aware of the damage sugar does and it is important you are able to remove it from your diet, or at least minimise it. There is also little to be gained by replacing sugar with sweeteners as these too have little benefit to your body, unless of course they are natural.

I have said nothing yet on the importance of drinking water, or at least water based fluids (excluding alcoholic drinks), and I hope each of you will be able to bear this in mind as this is something bodies are unable to live without. Consider the percentage of fluid in your body, which varies between fifty and eighty per cent, depending on age and gender, and then you may have an appreciation of how important it is to ensure you take in as much fluid as your body requires. There is a great deal of water within most of the foods you eat; however, it is still important you are able to drink too as this is needed to keep your body cleansed and hydrated.

So I think I have for the most part covered the aspects of caring for your body that I think are important, and I am hopeful it will be possible for you to implement any changes you feel are needed in order to have a greater level of care and respect for the body you have been given to live this life in.

7

The Reasons for Wishing to Incarnate on Earth

I have covered a portion of this subject previously; however, I would like to offer greater depth. Before you incarnate each of you spends a great deal of time deciding what it is you wish to achieve while on earth. It is important you are able to give yourself as much time as possible to ensure what you wish to achieve is achievable. There are a great many lessons it's possible to learn, and once these are learned you will be able to associate freely and easily with everybody in your soul group. This brings a great deal of freedom and openness, and means you are able to take a step further into enlightenment if that is your desire. Many spirits choose to take this step, and when they do it enables them to associate with a far greater number of people. It also means they are able to become more involved in the organisation that is spirit. A great many decisions are made in regard to how we, as a group, are able to progress our knowledge, and it is vital there are many people who are available to offer the benefit of their wisdom. It is important to us all that this organisation is particularly well run and so there are many committees and groups who work to ensure exactly that. These groups receive as much input from their members as possible before decisions are made in how it's possible for spirit to progress. It can often take a considerable length of time before all avenues are explored; however, it is a necessary process that needs to be undergone.

There are a large number of committees who are responsible for different aspects of spirit, and we work hard to try and ensure we are able to match the knowledge and skills of an individual to a particular committee. It may be a project is being developed and it is necessary to have the best minds possible for that project. We are also aware of the need to ensure your progress on earth passes in a way that is beneficial to you and us, and a great deal of discussion and implementation is undergone. We work to try and ensure that developments on earth are indeed for the benefit of those on earth. There is a considerable amount of development currently required and there are a number of committees who are working hard to try and ensure this is what happens.

How your incarnation can help progress your world

There has been, for many years, a considerable issue with the vibratory state that the earth finds itself in, as earth is for the most part out of sync with the rest of the universe. Much of this universe is divided into various levels of vibration and the only way it is possible for anything to enter into being is for it to be of a similar level of vibration, as every single thing that exists on your planet or elsewhere vibrates. The levels of vibration are divided up into what we call dimensions, and there are many dimensions. It is possible for there to be a number of dimensions existing in one place at one time, which is the reason why it's possible for many of us in spirit to be with you on earth and yet be unseen as we vibrate at a different rate to those who have chosen to walk the earth.

We fully understand this is a difficult concept, especially for those who are well educated, as we find they have often lost their ability to take on new concepts. We appreciate this is likely to be something that needs a good deal of thought as it is a difficult subject to grasp.

The entire universe you are currently occupying vibrates at a rate we choose to call the fifth dimension; however, earth vibrates at a rate that is within the fourth dimension. This has caused a great deal of friction over the years and it is something we have finally decided to correct.

We have been working towards this for decades and we are hopeful it will not be so much longer before we are able to make the final push and take your planet into the fifth dimension. A number of changes have already been undergone and your earth is progressing very nicely in this direction; however, there are still a number of changes that have yet to occur.

There is an unfortunate side effect to this change as earth needs to adjust her vibration, and in this period of adjustment it becomes necessary for many changes to occur within the earth as a whole. The effects of this, as many of you are observing, include changes to your weather patterns and it is likely that in the coming twenty years or so there will be rather more extreme changes in your weather. There are also likely to be a number of natural disasters. It is our belief that once this change has occurred your planet will begin to calm and the weather patterns and natural disasters will ease considerably; however, that is unlikely to occur for another twenty years or so, though it may be sooner.

We are aware this gives many of you a great deal of concern and worry, but we would like to reassure you this is a necessary part of the changes that will occur. It is likely many people will pass back to spirit when these extreme occurrences happen but we would like to reassure you all that all those who pass are prepared for their passing. We appreciate many of you will struggle to understand that; however, as we have discussed earlier, everybody when they choose to return to earth is given an exit date, so while it may not be something you are consciously aware of, on a deeper level you are fully aware of the date you will return to spirit. All of you who have chosen to remain on earth will in one way or another simply move yourselves away from the impending disaster. Your conscious minds will be unaware of this decision, although that is what will occur. We would like to advise all of you who are concerned about the upcoming disasters to remind yourselves that the only ones who will pass are the ones who are ready to pass, and when that occurs they will return to spirit. They will be accepted back with as much joy and celebration as anybody else who is returning to spirit.

Another effect of the need for your planet to alter its vibration is the need for the people who inhabit earth to elevate their own vibration. There is currently a great deal of disharmony occurring on your planet and it is important the level of harmony is increased. Many of you have concerns in regard to the number of wars currently occurring, and we are hopeful that in the not-too-distant future these will ease, and that during these wars many people who are unable to take on board the changes occurring in your world will be removed from your planet. We appreciate for some that will be difficult to grasp as we are aware many of you feel deeply for the struggles people are enduring in these wars, and while we agree with you, it is unfortunately something that needs to be passed through. We hope when this period of upheaval has passed there will be considerably fewer wars. In fact, we are hoping there will be no more war, although we appreciate that is a big step for your world.

So, it is important more people become aware of the need to change their attitudes and to try and become more open-minded and accepting of other people. There is no right or wrong way to live your life on earth, but it is important everybody is allowed to live the life they choose, provided of course they intend no harm to another living being. There is a great deal of freedom on your planet for this to occur, and it is important this is what happens.

How the changes in your world may affect you

It is likely in the coming years many people will struggle with these changes, and it is hoped that, with education and information, we from spirit are able to offer you a greater level of understanding that will be accepted by the people of earth. We in spirit have worked tirelessly to try and ensure there are a great many communicators between our world and yours to allow as many of you as possible to have a better understanding of the changes currently going on. It is additionally important to have as many people as possible who are open-minded and willing to change their attitudes and accept the differences between people in order to allow us to make these changes. In fact, these people need to be very much in the majority as it is not possible for this change in dimension to occur until such time as the people of earth are better adapted to living in the fifth dimension.

So not only will the natural disasters that occur remove many of the people who are of a less-than-developed nature, but it is also necessary for those who are more developed to spread their views and feelings to those around them. Do you see the work that needs to be undergone? I am aware for many of you this will be a very trying and difficult time but we would like to encourage you all to try and relax and accept what will occur. It is very much for the good of your planet and the people who live upon it.

When this change does eventually occur and your planet is able to step forward into the fifth dimension, the number of natural disasters will reduce considerably. This means your world will be in a position of ease and, instead of continuing levels of friction, which has been the case for millennia, it will calm considerably and life in your world will be easier. Not only will this have an effect on the people who live on earth, but we are also hoping that with the information and education we are able to offer there will be a change within them.

Within twenty years or so it is our hope that your world will become a very different place in which to live and many of you will find yourselves enjoying life considerably more than you currently do. Life will become easier and those of you who inhabit earth will be able to take on board a number of changes that have yet to come.

It is likely during this period of change there will be many upsets that occur between nations; however, as time continues it is our belief these upsets will gradually diminish. This is somewhat unfortunate but is something that needs to be endured, and it will pass, we can assure you of that.

We are giving you this information in the hope it will offer a greater level of understanding and will calm many of you. We are hopeful that throughout this period of change many will be accepting of these changes, and we also hope it will be possible for many of you to appreciate the differences between nations. It is important all of those who reside on earth are allowed to live their lives the way they choose, provided of course no suffering is inflicted on any living thing. It is important a greater level of respect is given not only to those who are unlike yourself, but also to everything that lives on your planet.

So, I think I have said enough for the time being in regard to the changes that will occur in your world, and I am hopeful it will be possible for you to give this a considerable amount of thought, as it is important that as many people as possible are able to adapt to these changes. There is a great deal more I could say on this subject and I think it's likely at a later point in this book I will do exactly that; however, for now it is important you are able to take on board what I have said.

8   How to Achieve What You Are on Earth to Achieve

You may believe I have covered this a few times already; however, there is more I would like to say on this subject.

I would like to advise you all of the importance of making the most of your time on earth. Many people have something of an inclination to sit back and wait for life to arrive at their door, and that, unfortunately, is not how things work; many of you would benefit greatly if you were to go out and *find* your life. For the most part it matters not what it is you choose to do; it is simply important your life on earth is as varied as possible. I appreciate for many that may prove to be something of a challenge as I am aware some of you have a great many concerns and fears that limit you in regard to the challenges you are able to offer yourself; however, there is little to be gained by hiding away from what you are there to achieve. If this is what happens, the next time you choose to return to earth the challenge you are presented with will be somewhat harder, so it is very much in your best interest to embrace the life you are there to live in the hope of achieving everything you are there to achieve.

A good number of you I feel sure will be struggling with that, as for many it is a challenge to know which direction you wish to take in your life; however, many of you have made efforts to take your life in a number of different directions and this is something I would really like to encourage you all to do. There is so much available to you and it's important to take on board any number of new challenges that appeal. It is easy to remain in the shelter of your own home and consider all the wonderful things that it's possible to do, but I would like to encourage each of you to step outside and embrace all that you feel you would like to do. Simply thinking of what you plan to do is not enough, it needs to be implemented, and I would encourage you to do exactly that.

Many of you have a significant number of lessons you are hoping to learn and it is important as many opportunities as possible are offered with this in mind. I am hopeful on completion of this book that this is exactly what you will do, given you are now aware of what it is you hope to achieve in this life.

As I have said previously, I am fully aware there are many of you with fears that limit your need to step out into the world, and I am hopeful this will make it easier to accomplish this task. I would like those of you who struggle with this to spend some time in quiet contemplation considering what you would like to experience. That can be in any number of forms, it is simply something that appeals, and I would then like to encourage you to imagine yourself in the thick of this endeavour. For many it may be necessary to imagine yourself immersed in this endeavour on a number of occasions in the hope of encouraging you to believe that this is in fact how your life is. I hope it will then prove to be somewhat easier to instigate proceedings to allow this to become part of your life. We have no wish here in spirit for you to do something that proves to be really rather frightening; however, I believe if you become accustomed to the types of challenges that will present to you in this particular scenario then it will be easier to take up the reins and enjoy what it is you wish to embrace. There will probably be a few periods when you regret the step forward, but it is likely these will be brief, and I hope you will all have a sense of achievement and a great deal of pleasure upon overcoming your fears and embracing this challenge.

It is extremely important many more of you are able to do exactly that as there are far too many who choose to hide behind fears and seem unable to learn and grow sufficiently, and that is of course why you chose to return to earth. I cannot emphasise enough how much you will appreciate that on your return to spirit. There are so many who arrive on earth, live a life and return home after a less-than-satisfactory attempt at what they were there to achieve; and there is often a great deal of disappointment and sadness involved in these cases. I say all this with your good intentions in mind and I cannot say it enough as so many people seem to be afraid to attempt much of anything.

I hope you feel inclined to consider this and embrace a desire to step out of your comfort zone and attempt a number of new challenges. I would, however, like to encourage you to attempt these challenges one at a time, as I suspect if you were to attempt more than one it would have the reverse effect and become really rather overwhelming, forcing you back into a sheltered existence.

There are a number of ways in which I think it may be possible to embrace this challenge, and one is to perhaps discuss with a friend the plans or challenges you are considering. I am of the belief that once your thoughts and feelings are out in the open it makes achievement considerably easier, as many of you have a tendency to bottle up your feelings or thoughts on particular subjects or people.

I have another suggestion, and that is to regularly set yourself a new challenge; how regularly rather depends on how big the challenge is. I am aware some of you may choose to change your job, in which case that may take a considerable amount of time; however, someone else may choose to purchase a new book to read or perhaps try their hand at a new skill, which may not necessarily take very long. If some of you felt inclined to make a pledge to perhaps embrace a new challenge regularly then this may encourage more of you to step outside your comfort zone. I strongly believe that once you accustom yourself to this it will become easier as you gradually realise many of your fears are all in your head. It is important when you are developing these new challenges that you are able to appreciate how well you are doing in your life. There is nothing to be gained by accepting these challenges and then criticising yourself for not being perfect.

Many of you have a voice within your head which seems intent upon crippling your desires, and it is that I would like to address next. I am unaware of where this rather critical voice comes from; however, it is something that many seem to spend much time listening to, and there is no need. All that happens as a result is your life becomes rather meaningless and many regrets develop due to challenges that are not taken up. It may be this critical voice of yours believes it is protecting you; however, that is simply not the case. It is something that has developed within your mind and needs very much to be silenced, and I have a suggestion for how to silence that voice. The next time you decide to step out of your comfort zone and your critical voice begins to limit you, try and tell yourself that this voice is ruining your life on earth and needs to be ignored. It may help to offer an affirmation of some kind that will speak of the positives within you, or it may be necessary for others to speak a little more harshly to this voice, and by that I mean criticise your critical voice, and I hope by doing this you will be able to quieten it. It may feel for a while as though there is a great deal of unrest going on in your head, but this will not last long. The point of the exercise is to make the voice go away and to encourage yourself to achieve any number of new challenges, big or small, that benefit your life, which is not possible when you have a critical voice in your head being rather destructive regarding your desires to learn and grow. It needs to be silenced. I am hopeful this will prove possible as this voice serves no good purpose for anybody; it is something that seems to have developed over the years in the minds of many and all it does is limit your ability to learn and grow. There is nothing to be gained from listening to this voice as all it does is paralyse people with fear, and that, quite frankly, is a complete waste of time.

I have another suggestion, and that is for those who have fears in regard to developing greater closeness in relationships, and those who wish to stand up for themselves. It is important to find ways to allow yourself to feel comfortable in the company of other people, and I would like to encourage you to try and adopt a policy of speaking to many more people throughout your day. This is a first step in becoming closer to other people, and also in being brave and standing up for yourself, but like many things in life it needs to start small. Simply allowing yourself to speak to as many people as possible throughout your day is a first step, and I would like to encourage you to do exactly that until you feel comfortable connecting with people in this way. I think if you are able to do that then the next step of taking relationships a little further will develop from there; it may take a while but it's necessary to begin that process in a small way, and while I appreciate the hardest part of that is the initial part, I believe when you become comfortable in speaking with many people it will become considerably easier to allow yourself to develop closer relationships. You see, it is necessary to change the energy that surrounds you, and for many there is something of a barrier in the ways you try to connect with other people. It is important more of you are able to connect with people freely and easily, and by doing that the barrier between you and others will gradually dissipate, and this, over time, will make it considerably easier to allow yourself to become closer to others. This will not happen overnight, in fact it may take a considerable period of time; it really depends on how high or thick the energy is that sits between you and the rest of the world. However, this is a very achievable way of giving you an opportunity in which to break down that barrier, and I cannot encourage you enough to get started as soon as you possibly can. I also think it is important, at the end of each day, to offer encouragement to yourself for speaking to any new people you have managed to speak to. There is nothing to be gained by offering any kind of negative feedback to yourself; it all needs to be positive, and by doing this, over time, your life will begin to change and you will find you have a number of relationships that are significantly deeper than the ones you previously had. They will also be greater in number.

For those who struggle to stand up for themselves, this too will improve, as often there is a belief that you are unworthy to be a friend or colleague of someone, or perhaps it's other people who behave in particular ways that cause you to feel less than able to stand up for yourself. The more people you are able to connect with, the more practice you are able to achieve in being in the company of many different types of people, and over time the experience you develop will allow you to stand up for yourself rather better than you currently do.

There are a number of ways to reinforce this behaviour in the hope of feeling stronger the next time you are in a position where you need to stand up for yourself. I have no wish for you to shout or retaliate against the behaviour of another person; however, it is important to stand up for yourself and your beliefs, and I believe for many that will become somewhat easier if you are able to feel more secure and safe in the knowledge that you have many people who are willing to be there for you. It may be the next time you need to stand up for yourself they are not around; however, I would like to suggest you try and imagine all of them standing with you. This may take some practice, but it is important you are able to find a way, no matter how small, of allowing all the people you appreciate and whose company you enjoy to stand with you in the hope of giving you the opportunity to stand strong and be the person you wish to be, and that is someone who is able to stand firm in their beliefs and who is able to be strong and speak their truth to whoever chooses to challenge that.

Everybody on earth is equal, there is nobody who is superior or inferior to anyone else, and it is important to remember that. Those of you who choose to be unkind to others or to force your feelings or beliefs on other people are simply doing that for reasons of your own. There is no truth at all in your belief that you are any better than anyone else. You are all equal in the eyes of God and that is how you will remain forever. It is curious so many of you believe there is a hierarchy on earth, as that is simply not the case. Any belief you have that anybody else is better or lesser than you is all in your mind, and time needs to be spent on that thought in the hope of destroying it. Earth would be a far kinder place if more people were able to dispel this thought, as there is no truth to it whatsoever.

I think that is all I intended to say on that particular subject, and I am hopeful that this chapter has offered an insight into how it's possible to develop your life in ways that previously were not available to you.

9 How to Enjoy the Life You Live on Earth

I think it is important I offer a few clues to make this journey easier as I am aware many people struggle with how to enjoy their time on earth.

We in spirit fully appreciate time on earth is not easy, and the majority of people who choose to return think long and hard about what it is they can achieve when they are there. Time spent on earth is not considered to be easy as there are so many chores that need to be accomplished simply to survive, and while we accept there is no memory of what life can be like without chores, we appreciate nonetheless that this life is an arduous one. So, I would like to make a number of suggestions regarding how to enjoy life on earth as I do not believe it takes much thought and energy to enjoy this time.

My first suggestion is to encourage you to try and look on the positive side of life. So many choose to focus on the negative, and that unfortunately means that is what you are drawing your attention to. It means the negative side of life becomes your focus, and it may be that any number of positive things are occurring around you, but because your focus is on the negative, that is all you are able to see and be aware of. In this instance the solution is fairly straightforward; it is simply to alter the focus of your life. Instead of focusing on the negative aspects, try and focus on the positive ones. This will require a little time; however, with some effort it can be achieved in a few days. By spending your time focusing on all the positive aspects of your life you will lift your spirit considerably. Who really wishes to spend their life wallowing in negativity? For many it has simply become a habit, but habits can be altered and that is what I would like to encourage you to do. No matter how miserable a person's life is, there are always positive aspects within it, and if you are able to focus on those aspects you will find positivity will be drawn to you, and over the period of a few days it will be possible to embrace the more positive aspects of your life. This life is hard enough without making it any harder than it needs to be, and simply by altering your focus your life will be considerably easier.

I would also like to suggest to you the importance of appreciating all you have in your life. I feel sure some of you will argue there is nothing in your life that's worth appreciating; however, that is simply not the case as everybody has things within their life it's possible to appreciate. All it requires is an opportunity to refocus your thoughts and consider the benefits of many of the things you have. Simply to have a roof over your head, for instance, is something worth appreciating. It may leak and the rain may pour through, but you do nonetheless have a roof on your house, and that is how it's possible to appreciate the things in your life.

I would like you to take another look at your life and work hard to find the positive aspects of it. It may be important for some to take a few negative aspects and flip those around to make a positive view; for instance, a person may say how disappointed they are that the friend they believed they had was in fact an enemy, and the positive way to view that would be to show a level of appreciation that your friend is choosing to demonstrate their true self. Or you may wish to consider the importance of having only kind and gentle people within your life and to appreciate that this person no longer fits that criteria, and so acknowledge their kindness in demonstrating their lack of desire to fall within it. Do you see? Everything has a positive side if you choose to embrace it. I appreciate there are times when life can be so miserable it is extremely difficult to focus on the positive; however, provided a significant portion of your life is given to considering the positive aspects of your world, then on the occasions when life becomes miserable it will not be quite so encompassing.

How important it is to be aware of how your friends reflect your positivity (or lack thereof)

It is important for all of you to have a number of people within your life. It may be your life is currently passing through a particular phase, in which case the people you are able to attract are likely to be going through a similar phase in their lives; however, once that phase has passed it will be possible to attract any number of other people who are in a similar position to yourself. It may be you find yourself surrounded by people who are not helping you move away from a particular scenario that is playing out in your life, and in these instances it is important to make that move yourself. Once you have instigated that move you will find yourself attracting people who are at a similar stage in their lives, and so life becomes somewhat easier. Do you see how important it is to put yourself in a place where you are able to attract people of a similar standing in life? It enables you to break free from the negativity that was breeding within your life and amongst the friends or colleagues you were attracting. Life is very much within your control, if you are only able to understand your part in what it is you are attracting.

Many people on earth have a sense that life happens to them, and that is not the case; each of you is very much in control of your own destiny, and if you are unhappy with the situation you find yourself in, then alter it. It may be you need to change the situation, or that you simply need to alter your viewpoint. Some of you, I am sure, feel extremely stuck in your life, but all of you have options to deal with that. You all have a great deal of control over your lives; it is simply how you choose to express that control – and I would like to make a few suggestions regarding how to do that.

One way to alter your place in this world is simply to move. Once you have reached adulthood you have the power to change your situation, and if you find yourself in a place that is impossibly hard and unbearable then you have that option. It may prove to be extremely hard to accomplish but nonetheless that is an option available to you.

There are others who are happy with their living conditions but struggle with the people around them, and it may be a change in work is required, or an attitude change on your part in order to begin attracting people who are of a higher vibration. When I say that, I mean people who are lighter in nature, the kind of people who find life easier. They are the ones who have learned to embrace the positivity of life, and to be amongst these kinds of people makes your own life easier. It is important for all of you who are trying to improve the conditions of your life to work hard to find ways to look at your life in a far more positive manner, and gradually you will be able to observe not only how much easier you feel, but also how much nicer the people are that surround you. It may be that as a result of the negativity and unpleasantness that surrounds you, you have chosen to become something of a hermit, and this will never do as all of us are designed to mix with other people. In the long term, becoming a hermit leads to a rather miserable existence, and so it is important to step outside your home and begin connecting with people.

You may be confined to your home due to a disability of some kind, in which case work to connect with charities or groups who are willing to offer a helping hand to either come and help you visit others, or come and visit you themselves. These are options that are open to you; it simply needs your participation to make the most of them.

Recurring situations

There are those of you who work hard to try and find groups of positive people but somehow continue to find groups of negative people instead. It may be that they seem on the surface to be positive but over time their negativity comes to the fore. So I have a suggestion, and that is to try and find a way of continuing to view these people in a positive light. It is likely, if this continues to happen, that one of two things keeps occurring. One is the possibility that there is a lesson to be learned, and I have covered this in a previous chapter; however, it is also possible that the groups in which you find yourself are either tainted by your own negativity, or you find it difficult to observe whether or not they are initially positive or negative. It may be that due to a need to find positive people you find groups of people who appear positive and then over time clearly are not. In these instances I would like to encourage you to consider your part in this scenario. It may be your own negativity is drawing these people towards you; however, it may also be a question of desperation on your part that means you are only able to see their positive aspects initially and fail to observe the negative parts of their personalities, in which case it is important to learn that all of us have negative and positive aspects to our personalities. The only way to be with people who are the same as you is to consider yourself to be a mirror, which means you are attracting the people who are like yourself. We all of us make mistakes at times; however, if this mistake becomes consistent then it's important to look to yourself and understand why this keeps happening. I am aware for many of you that may prove to be a rather arduous task to accomplish, but I would like you to be as objective as you can in the hope of gaining a greater level of understanding. When you have achieved that understanding and choose to implement the suggestions I have made I feel sure your life will change considerably.

There are people who spend their life believing they are a victim of circumstance, but that is simply not the case. Each of you is very much in control of your own life; it simply requires a level of understanding and a change in view to make your life considerably better. Do you see? I hope so, as this slight alteration in your perspective on the world can improve your life considerably, and the opportunity to do that is in your hands.

How important it is to take control of your life

No one on earth is there to be a victim of the circumstances that are doled out to them. Each of you needs to find a way to alter the circumstances around you, and I am hopeful that in this part of the book you will find a few extra insights into how to have the power to change your circumstances. I appreciate this may not be something that children or teenagers are able to embrace; however, for those who have reached an age of maturity you are indeed able to embrace the changes I am about to suggest.

If you find yourself in circumstances that are harsh or less than comfortable, I would like to urge you to examine the reasons you believe you are unable to alter your situation; the reasons that bind you to the situation you are currently in. Many of you will find the reasons that hold you in a particular place are based on fear and the belief that life is easier when it's familiar, and that is not the case. It is important for all of you to be brave, to step outside your comfort zone and work to implement changes that will lift you out of a less than beneficial place. I appreciate for many this will be particularly arduous, as the fears that bind you to a place are often overwhelming. These do, however, need to be pushed through; in fact they need to be pushed out of the way in order to allow you to take up the mantle and begin taking your life in the direction you wish to go. Each of you has the strength and the power to do this for yourself. It is simply a matter of recognising and accepting that that is the case. Many find yourselves in situations that are less than satisfactory and choose to remain there, and there is no need. In fact, it is of the utmost importance that you find the strength to alter the surroundings that encompass you in order to grow and learn from your experiences. When people find themselves in a situation that is less than pleasing many will gradually find ways of adjusting to that situation, and the only way to do that is to find ways to accept it. That is done by placing restrictions on your personality – by that I mean choosing to ignore parts of your personality that are important. It is as if a brick is placed on parts of you in order to prevent yourself from examining that part of your personality, and yet you are all truly magnificent beings; none of you should be in a position to limit how you feel about anything. The personality that you are is unique and needs to be celebrated rather than masked. Do you see how important it is for you to be in situations where you are able to fully embrace the person you are? To find yourself in a situation where you need to hide parts of your personality is no good for anyone, and you will find over time that this will become a bigger and bigger problem, so it is important to find a way to remove yourself from that situation. It is essential all of you are able to embrace all aspects of yourselves, even the dark parts, as there are many positive aspects to the darker side of our personalities.

When you find yourself in a position where you are able to alter your situation it will be difficult for a while not to reproduce the surroundings you are used to, because it is likely that once you have managed to remove yourself to a different place you will continue behaving in a particular way, and unfortunately that has the effect of reproducing a similar situation to that which previously surrounded you. So it's important to ensure you alter your behaviour as well as your surroundings. This is what will give you the best chance of improving your situation. It is also difficult to make such sweeping changes all in one go, but it is possible, and I would like to encourage all of you to be aware of the importance of altering not only your position in life, but also your reaction to it. It is essential a full understanding of your part in reproducing similar scenarios is embraced.

I would now like to say something about how important it is to embrace the possibility that you are the driver of your own car, and the opportunities this puts before you are endless. Each of you has an endless number of opportunities presented to you but many have become so stuck in a rut it seems impossible to recognise them. In fact, there are many instances when we listen to you complain about the situation you find yourself in and yet right in front of you are opportunities to change your circumstances. We find that rather frustrating as we work hard to ensure opportunities are provided and often this does not appear to be recognised. I would like to suggest to you all that you open your minds a little and view your lives with a greater sense of adventure, and perhaps be able to embrace changes that surround you rather than accept your lot. Do you see and understand how easy it can be to simply alter the circumstances you find yourself in if you do not feel they work particularly well for you? It may be that compromises are required; however, there are always opportunities available if you find yourself in a situation that no longer appeals.

That is all I will say on that subject, and I hope many of you will be able to give this chapter some of your time and try and understand why the situations you find yourselves in are very much of your own making.

10 How to Embrace All Your World Has to Offer

Again, I am sure many will feel I have covered this topic a few times already; however, there is more I would like to add as I think it is important as many people as possible are given as many tools as possible in order to make the most of their life on earth. It is crucial people are aware of the reason they are there and how to make the most of their time. So, in that vein I would like to offer some more information about how to make that possible.

Firstly, I would like to spend a little time going over what I have said up till now, which is that I hope it will be possible for many of you to view your life in a different light and perhaps galvanise yourself into action in the hope of exploiting as many opportunities that are offered to you as possible. I would also like it if more of you were able to alter your attitudes in the hope of achieving a slightly different view of your life, and as a result enjoy yourself more.

I would like to point out to you the knowledge I have offered in regard to what happens on your death in the hope that many will have less fear of what comes next and also less fear of living your life. I am aware for some of you the fear of dying inhibits how you live your life and I am hopeful that, emboldened with this knowledge, it will be easier to make the most of your life. This journey on earth is meant to be a time of enjoyment and it is important as many of you as possible are able to embrace that. It is also important as many of you as possible are able to exploit the opportunities offered to learn your lessons.

I would now like to encourage you to make the most of your time on earth, and I will start by advising you that it is important for all of you to feel sufficiently emboldened to allow yourself to step forward and embrace the life you have and to make the most of what this world has to offer, which is indeed bounteous. There are so many who choose to hide away and simply exist, and yet there is so much available to you. This is a time of opportunity, and for many a time when you are able to make the most of your life. I cannot stress that enough as there really is so much that's available to you, yet there are so many who choose not to take those opportunities and the reason they are not taken up is fear. This fills us with sadness and disappointment as that is not something which is an issue here in spirit. We appreciate you have physical bodies that can be damaged; however, they can also be repaired, and on the occasions when they are damaged beyond repair we will step forward and do our best to ensure a greater level of healing occurs. We feel sure many will have heard of cases where people have been healed and doctors are dumbfounded as to how that happened, and we would like to advise you that it is in fact us, and when I say 'us' I mean either spirit or the angelic realm, who step forward to try and ensure it is possible for you to heal.

There are those amongst you who are aiming for learning associated with sickness or injury, and in those instances we are unable to improve your healing until such time as the lesson has been learned. Having said that, there are also some of you who are there to teach others, and it may be your illness or injury is for exactly that purpose, in which case a level of learning is required on the part of your carer, and please remember this is something you have agreed to before you incarnated on earth. There is nobody on earth who has been given this task without prior consent; that simply never happens. I would encourage you to remember that life is very different in spirit and many decisions are made here that we think would not have been made on earth as the information available to us is considerably greater. There is also a much greater awareness of the continuity of life, as in spirit we are all aware we have been here for millennia and our time on earth is extremely brief. I appreciate that is not necessarily how you feel, but in the scheme of things it is extremely brief. Time in spirit has a very different perspective to time on earth.

How to enjoy your life more than you currently do

I think it is important more of you have a better grasp of the need to enjoy yourself while you are on earth. I have spoken already of how important it is for this to be the case in the hope of lightening your energy and minimising the negative aspects of earth; however, there is more I can add.

For some of you there is a belief that your time on earth needs to be taken rather seriously and, in many ways, you are correct. However, for many that seriousness seems to obliterate your need for fun, and I hope what I am about to say will dispel those beliefs.

For those of you who are intent upon having a rather serious life I would like you to try and consider how to make greater efforts in enjoying yourself. It is of the utmost importance that you are able to place a much higher value on fun and pleasure, and I encourage you to do this in the hope you will be able to incorporate more fun into your life. More fun gives you more opportunities to steer your life in the direction it needs to go. It is during times of fun that your energy undergoes a considerable change, and it is then that we are able to have closer contact with you and send your life in directions you may not yet have thought of. On these occasions many of us are able to get together and do our best to try and influence you in how your life would benefit from taking certain paths. We have a great deal of knowledge of how it's possible for people to enjoy their lives and we have had a great many discussions with you about how you wish to enjoy your life on earth, and so we work extremely hard to try and ensure your wishes are adhered to. We also try to ensure you have as many opportunities as possible to achieve this. It may seem difficult to understand how that is possible and I would struggle considerably if I were to try and advise you on how we manage that, but that is in fact what happens. I also think it's important that more of you not only give fun a greater value in your life, but are also willing to make it a greater portion of your life. No one is on earth to work constantly; that is not the point of being there at all.

It may be you love the work you do, in which case it may be harder to step away and have other forms of fun; it is necessary, however, that this is what happens. It is important to have a variety of fun within your life, and to have a variety of people who are associated with each form of fun. We would like to encourage each of you to have as many friends and colleagues as possible; by having various forms of fun there is often a different group of people associated with each. This means you are afforded a great many opportunities to learn what it is you are on earth to learn. Do you see how the two are closely intertwined? Learning and growing and having a great deal of fun are really the only things you are there for, nothing else, and it is vital a greater level of focus is placed upon that.

It is difficult to make learning and growing a priority as when this does occur it is generally through our efforts that it ends up being presented to you. We offer you this advice in the hope you are able to see how possible it is to achieve all the things you are there to achieve. Each of you has made a big decision to spend time on earth and it is important you feel able to get the most from it; the joy and pleasure people feel on their return home when they have achieved what they were there to achieve is truly immense, especially when so many of you spend a great many lives trying to achieve the same thing, as there really is no need. We are hopeful that by offering you this information and doing our best to try and spell out how possible it is to make the most of your life, you will do exactly that, and that this will limit the number of lives many of you need to participate in, when really all that was needed was a greater level of knowledge about your reasons for being there.

It is unfortunate that, when you incarnate on earth and it becomes necessary to remove memories of previous lives, your reasons for being there and your aims for your life are removed at the same time. If it was possible for that not to be the case then that is what we would do; however, we have tried a great many ways to offer you this information and also to try and leave this information with you, but to date all have achieved a lesser level of success than we would have hoped. So, we now find ourselves offering you this information with the hope that you will embrace what we are saying and use it to make more of your life.

We are aware there are a number of attempts by people to share this information with you and we are pleased with the efforts that are being made; however, it is important this information is spread to as many people across the globe as possible as there really are so many who choose to live a less-than-fulfilling life.

We are also aware many of you are embroiled in religions that make embracing the idea of spiritualism rather difficult, and we do understand, that is the reason we have made so little reference to God, as we think for those of you who embrace different religions it may be better for us to avoid the subject. There is, however, one thing we would like to say on that subject, and that is that there is only one God and the ways people choose to address their God are the ways of man. Any religion that is adopted is acceptable, unless of course it causes any suffering to any person or living thing; as we have said before, this is unacceptable. I think it is important many more of you have a greater appreciation of the fact that there is one God who watches over us all and his presence is everywhere all of the time. I say 'his' but I could say 'her'; it is difficult to be specific. In many ways religion has its place in your world and we have no wish to prevent any of you from spending time with your beliefs, except of course those who choose to cause harm. You are all there to make the most of your life and to be allowed the freedom to do so.

It is important, I think, for many more of you to have a greater level of acceptance of other people and their beliefs. Simply because a person has a different religion or viewpoint on the world to you is no excuse to cause them any upset or harm. Each of you needs to have a greater respect for all those who surround you. Everybody on earth has the right to their opinion even though some may appear to be very different from your own. Each of you is there to live the life you chose before you incarnated and it is important that is what happens; it is not the place of any one of you to prevent anybody else from doing that. I believe if more of you were able to embrace a far greater acceptance of other people and their beliefs, your world would be a far more comfortable place for you all to live in. It is simply a waste of time to spend any of your energy on limiting what others choose to do. What others choose to do is entirely down to them and none of your business (excluding those who have committed a crime) and that needs to be remembered.

Differences are something to be embraced on earth and not something that need to be shunned or ridiculed. Do you see how you are all there for different reasons and it is important you are all able to live your lives in different ways in order to achieve what it is you are there to achieve? I hope that is clear.

Embracing the differences between you

There will always be a level of upset between people who are trying to achieve the same thing but have different ways to achieve it, and a greater respect needs to be offered to each other with this in mind. But how is it possible to achieve a good result when both people feel their input has value? Well, I have a suggestion by which I hope to offer you a level of enlightenment, and that is for more of you to be in a position to offer your suggestions freely and openly, and to give your time to listen to someone else's opinions. Frequently all an individual needs is to be heard. It is often the case that disharmony occurs when one person wishes to enforce their opinions on someone else in order for their ideas to move forward; however, if people were able to allow both to speak freely and openly then for the most part the problems would disappear as it often becomes clear which of the two is presenting the most workable solutions. It is important each person is able to be honest and open with their thoughts, and that the solution is about finding the best result rather than one person's thoughts being placed above another's. A greater level of appreciation needs to be gained for the aim of the project, and by that I mean people being open to accepting the best solution rather than 'their' solution. We appreciate that is not always possible as there are many amongst you who are intent on enforcing your ideas on everyone. We are hopeful that over time this need will diminish, especially with the changes that are occurring in your world.

How to spend more time in the company of others

Amongst you are those who believe they are unworthy of spending time with other people, and by this I mean those with beliefs that others have no wish to share their time with them. Firstly, I would like to point out this is a belief rather than a fact, and also that for the most part it is a decision the person has made on their own with no input from anyone else, so it follows the information is rather flawed. For those of you who have shied away from mixing with others for a while and have become somewhat quieter than you would typically be, it is important to step forward a number of times in order to overcome the behaviour that has resulted from your lack of sociability. It may be the group you are working to associate with is one that would benefit from the company of other people, or it may be that a better group is available for you to join. It is important each of you is with a group of people that are similar to you in the hope of having a stronger sense of bonding with them. It is simply no good having a belief that you belong to a particular group of people while having no sense of connection with them. It is for this reason I would like to encourage you to seek out people who have similar interests to you, as that is often the glue that holds a group together. Simply having a desire to belong to a group because they have greater status is a waste of your time. Do you see how important it is to find people who share your interests, as that will bind you together?

For some of you it may prove somewhat difficult to find groups of people who share your interests. It may be a great deal of work is required on your part, but this is the age of technology when most of us are connected to each other. While we wish to encourage more of you to spend considerably less of your time with technology, we are also able to appreciate it has a number of advantages, and where your interests are somewhat unique, that is where technology will come into its own and afford you the opportunities to find people who are like yourself. I would like to point out you still need to have as much face-to-face contact as possible, so it is far more beneficial to find those who are like yourself and then meet them in person, and to perhaps only use the technology to find like-minded groups.

Our concerns in regard to technology

In many ways the technology in your world has a great deal to offer, and we have no wish to limit the technology you have available to you; in fact we have on a number of occasions offered suggestions regarding how it can be improved. I do, however, have considerable concern that for many, so much time is spent connected to your handheld devices and your computers, as your lives on earth need to be spent with people. We have no wish for any of you to spend huge amounts of time connected to these devices, and it is important you all live in the real world rather than a virtual one. To be connected to a virtual world for so many hours every day cuts you off from the interactions that are occurring around you, and these interactions need to occur as they are the building blocks for the connections and relationships within your life. It is important as many connections as possible are made person to person, as this is the way relationships are formed and allowed to grow. How many times have you sent a message to someone else only for them to feel hurt or upset by it, when your intention was completely different? That is unfortunately what happens, and this needs to be avoided.

11 How to Achieve Your Aims

Again, you may believe I have covered this previously; however, there are a few things I would like to add.

It is important while on earth to focus on what it is you desire to achieve. I fully appreciate the vast majority of you have no clue why you are on earth, or at least what it is you hope to achieve, and I would like to offer an understanding about how to make the most of situations where there is an opportunity to learn and grow and for you to achieve your aims. Each of you is offered many opportunities to learn what you came to learn, and it's important you have a better understanding of when those opportunities occur. I appreciate many of you have no idea when these opportunities present themselves, and I feel that in order to achieve a greater level of learning it is easier if you are aware of when a scenario is being presented. The times when the greatest learning can be achieved are for the most part the times in your life that are something of a struggle. It may be many of you are aware of enduring a particular struggle throughout your life, and it is there that the learning can be found.

As we have discussed in previous chapters, your response needs to vary each time these events are presented to you, in the hope of achieving your aims. It is important to be on the alert so that when these scenarios present you are able to react in a different way, and it is necessary for you to have a good understanding of the ways in which you have previously responded. So, I would like to suggest, the next time you find yourself in a scenario that has presented to you a number of times in the past, that you sit and consider your earlier responses in the hope of ensuring that a different response is offered on this occasion. It is likely that when you choose to respond in a different way you will find yourself feeling extremely uncomfortable, and this is because it is necessary to step outside your comfort zone. This tends to cause discomfort as it is something that is completely new to you. It is my hope that the next time you are able to respond in a different way it will be the response required for that particular lesson, and once the correct response has been given this scenario will never present to you again. It is important to remember each scenario has a level of difficulty attached to it; each time it is presented and a lack of success occurs, it means that on the next occasion the lesson will be somewhat harder in the hope you will achieve the learning.

For some of you a particular lesson has been attempted throughout many lifetimes, which means that each time it is presented there is a greater level of difficulty. I am hopeful some of you will be able to grasp the reason why some people's lives are extremely difficult, and some can start out difficult and then suddenly become rather easy. (I feel sure some of you will have observed this in the lives of others.) The reason this occurs is because what they were there to learn has suddenly been learned and the pressure is off. It may be that in a subsequent life they choose to learn other lessons, but for now that need is not quite so strong.

Many people on their return to earth choose to learn more than one lesson and these can be presented to you at random, there is no fixed order, so the ease of your life depends on how many of these lessons you manage to learn. I am hopeful that, armed with this knowledge, you are able to observe many of your earlier struggles from a fresh perspective, and that with this awareness subsequent lessons will be somewhat easier. They may of course need to be presented a number of times, but being aware that this is what is occurring does make the learning somewhat easier; at least that is my belief.

So now you are aware of how these lessons present to you I hope to provide you with some understanding of how to make the most of them, and by that I mean how you can grow as a result, as there is a little more involved than simply learning.

It is important you are able to take on board what you have learned in the hope of allowing yourself to grow. So the next time a lesson presents and a different response is provided, you may find yourself in the position of having achieved a level of learning, and having learned a particular lesson it is important to apply that to how you live your life, or how you live your life in response to other people. It may be that during the learning you were able to achieve a greater understanding of the behaviour of others, and it is important throughout the rest of your life to have a greater awareness for the struggles of other people. Do you see how important it is to actually *use* your learning, as it is there that growth is achieved? If a person were to learn and understand a particular lesson but felt unable to use it in their life, either for themselves or for the benefit of others, then it is an indication that growth has not actually occurred, and after a while it will become necessary for the learning to present itself again.

Time is always given to people in the hope an understanding of what they have learnt will gradually permeate their mind, and growth has the opportunity to occur. It is important they are given this time as there are many who need a while to take on board what they have learned. We are unclear of the reason for that as in theory it should be employed as soon as the learning occurs, but that does not seem to be the case; there are a great many of you who seem to need a period of time for this understanding to be accepted and employed. There are also a few who choose not to use this learning and unfortunately need to have the scenario presented again. There is a level of sadness on our part when this occurs, although it does not tend to occur very often. It is important all of you achieve your growth as this really is part of the learning process and provides excellent evidence to us that the learning has indeed been achieved.

How to appreciate the amount of learning you have achieved

While we appreciate it is extremely difficult to understand the learning you have undertaken and achieved, and also the amount of growth that has been attained, it is nonetheless in your interest at various points throughout your life to take time out and consider the person you were at, perhaps, fifteen. Then reflect back on your life in periods from that date and try to become more aware of the changes that have occurred throughout that time in the hope of getting a grasp of what it is you have been able to learn and grow from. It may be you feel there is little difference, in which case it is important to focus on your learning. It may be that during your life you have chosen to respond in similar ways to the opportunities that have been presented to you, in which case little learning has been achieved. However, it may be you feel like a completely different person to the one you were at, say, fifteen, in which case a great deal of learning has occurred, and I commend you for your ability to respond in so many different ways in order to achieve your lessons and the subsequent growth. There will be a great deal of celebration on your return home when you are able to appreciate the amount of growth you have achieved.

Once this has been achieved and all your lessons have been learned there is very little need to return to earth. Some do because they enjoy their time there; however, there are many more of you who choose not to return and to spend the remainder of your time in spirit, as for most, the trials and tribulations that are part of time on earth prove to be too much without a good reason for enduring them. It is necessary to work extremely hard throughout your time on earth as there are so many chores that are necessary in order to sustain life. The differences in our lives in spirit are huge as we are freed from many of these chores, and as we have no need to sleep, our days are considerably longer. For some that proves to be something of a struggle and by returning to earth their days are rather broken up; and there are some who choose to return because they would prefer to take a break from living in spirit, but these people are extremely few in number.

It may be that someone in spirit has a particular job we have requested them to do when they return to earth and they may have achieved all the lessons they need to learn, and so their life on earth appears to be somewhat easier than most. However, they are there to perform a particular task for us and, for the most part, for the benefit of mankind. As there are few reasons we choose to request a person to return to earth, it tends to be that they are needed to provide a greater level of learning to those on earth, or to implement a particular project that we feel would benefit earth. There have been a number of instances of this throughout your history; however, these people really are few and far between. There may in fact be only a handful that this applies to. Each of you needs to note that the likelihood of this scenario applying to you is remarkably small, as we are aware there are many who believe they are there to fulfil a particular task, and while this may be true it is extremely unlikely you are the only person who can perform that task.

There are times when we are concerned for the way your planet is progressing and we feel it pertinent to ensure there are a number of people who are able to perhaps guide your planet in the direction we desire, which I would like to add is always for the benefit of those on earth. In those instances, we ensure there are a considerable number of people who are able to fulfil that task. This is important to us as nobody is there to do exactly as we bid and it may be that during your life a decision is made not to pursue what we hoped you would. It is your decision. It is for that reason we have a number of backup plans in the form of others who are sufficiently developed to undertake that particular task. It may of course be that they all choose not to pursue the aims they came to pursue, in which case we need to think again and we have a number of other options open to us.

So you see, even though you may feel a pull to perform a particular type of work, it is necessary to understand it is by no means compulsory. Your life on earth is very much your own and is there to be enjoyed in the way you choose to enjoy it, provided no suffering is inflicted on anyone or anything in the process. I hope you now understand how important it is to do as you wish in the pursuit of learning, growing and enjoying yourself.

How to achieve your aim to be the person you are on earth to be

This is currently very much a catchphrase, 'to be the person I came here to be', and that is something I would like all of you to work hard to be, as that too is part of your learning and growth. In spirit it is easy to be just who we wish to be; however, given the number of fears and challenges people are faced with on earth there is a tendency for your lives to become somewhat smaller than they need to be, and it is important each of you works to alter that scenario and try to expand your world in the hope of becoming the person you wished to be before you arrived on earth. There are a great many opportunities for all of you to expand your learning and growth, and as this is undergone it becomes possible for you to gain greater levels of confidence. By achieving that, most people are able to become the person they hope to be. There are some who choose to walk a different path, and as their learning progresses, make decisions to step away from the human race and immerse themselves in their spiritual development. While this has a great many benefits it also has a great many disadvantages as it means your world becomes somewhat smaller and you are no longer able to continue in your aim of becoming the person you intended to be. Instead of associating with a great many people and enjoying yourself, your life becomes one of introspection. As a result, the enjoyment you are there to experience is no longer available, and that is not why you are there. There is in fact nobody on earth who is there to spend their life in introspection and fail to embrace the enjoyment that is available. I appreciate there are not so many who choose to walk this path; however, there are a few and I would like to try and dispel the myth that by pursuing this life you are somehow becoming more spiritual, as that simply is not the case.

People who are more spiritually developed are able to appreciate life and enjoy all that it has to offer. They are able to pursue the things that give them a great deal of pleasure, as we are able to connect with them considerably easier than with those who choose a life of introspection.

It means we are able to encourage them to pursue any aims they wish to achieve. That may not necessarily be in regard to learning and growth; it may be an individual has a desire to learn a particular skill or achieve something, and when they are pursuing the path of enjoyment we are able to guide and encourage them to achieve what they hoped to achieve on this particular journey. It may be that their aim was to achieve something for the benefit of mankind; however, it is necessary to have opportunities made available to us to allow us to guide them, and this can only occur when the person enjoys themself or is pursing hobbies that give them a great deal of fun. So, do you understand the importance of fun in your life? This is something I cannot stress enough as so many seem to feel that fun and enjoyment are for when everything else has been achieved, and this is not the case. They are a very necessary part of your life, throughout your life. All that is required is for them not to become the bulk of your life, as balance is particularly important.

The importance of being able to embrace the fun in your life

I hope up till now I have made it clear how important fun and enjoyment are to each and every one of you. However, it's important I spend a little time focusing on ways to find the fun and enjoyment in your life. I have previously discussed how important I think it is to look to your childhood, at least those of you who were able to enjoy your childhood, to find things that pleased you when you were young so you can try and return to them as an adult. However, that does not always work and I would like to make a few suggestions as to how to find things that please you.

I would like you to consider for a while the things in your life that have given you a great deal of pleasure, and while you are doing that to try and understand what it was about them that pleased you. It may be you particularly enjoyed watching the pleasure on the faces of other people, or it may be that the laughter you experienced was so profound you would like to experience it again. There may be any number of reasons you enjoyed a particular task, and when you have thought about that I would like you to try and find ways to implement that pleasure in your life. It may be that an entirely new pursuit begins with the aim of achieving that pleasure. It may be you choose to do exactly what you did previously. It matters not so long as you are able to find ways that offer you greater levels of fun and enjoyment. It is of the utmost importance each of you find ways to have these experiences in your life, and on as regular a basis as possible.

There are many who choose to spend their life caring for animals and this is perfectly acceptable; lives do not need to be spent in the pursuit of caring for others in one way or another. The options available to you are as broad as you can possibly imagine. There is of course one stipulation, and that is to cause no suffering to anybody or anything, which, as we have said previously, is completely unacceptable. I hope many of you are now considering all the options it's possible for you to employ. For those whose lives are really busy, this task is likely to be something of a trial, and it may be you need to be particularly creative in order to find ways to introduce fun to your life. For those who have large families much of your enjoyment may be achieved simply by caring for your children; however, that is not always the case. There are many who struggle considerably in bringing up a family and it is especially important to find ways to step outside of your family and enjoy yourself. There are many ways this can be achieved; however, one must be particularly tenacious in order to do so as there are not so many opportunities to find carers who are willing to care for your children while you go off and enjoy yourself. Nonetheless, they are there; it simply requires greater focus, and of course, it is always possible to ask us to help in any way we can, but we need to be asked and to be given time to accomplish that task. So you see your life is very much in your own hands and simply needs focus on your part to guide you in the direction you choose.

12 The Learning Available from a Life in Turmoil

You may believe I have covered this before; however, there is more I feel I can add. Firstly, I would like to begin by briefly covering what I have already said by talking to you about the importance of embracing all the opportunities offered to you in the hope of learning and subsequently growing.

Throughout your life a great many opportunities are offered to you and it is important as many of these as possible are taken up in the hope of achieving your aims for being on earth. I am aware for many this causes a great deal of upset as these opportunities are intended to teach you, and it is simply not possible for that to occur when your life is bobbing along in a very easy manner. If it were then we would all be able to do our learning while in spirit, but that is not the case. A great deal of learning is undertaken when your life is in turmoil, and it may be you have recognised how many young people's lives are somewhat tumultuous and then, as they reach middle or older age, seem to calm. The reason for this is that we like to offer you as many opportunities as possible to learn and grow, and as the learning is achieved it is less necessary to bombard you with so many opportunities. If you find your life continues into middle age in a state of turmoil then it may be important to consider how you react to these scenarios. If you find yourself responding in the same way each time then that may well be the reason these experiences are continuing to be offered to you, as there is no learning involved when people respond in the same way. I appreciate it takes a great deal of courage on your part to continually respond in different ways, as it requires you to step outside your comfort zone. This means responding in ways that people around you are unfamiliar with, and not only is there a level of discomfort involved for you in reacting in a way that is unlike anything you have done before, but you will very likely find those around you will be expressing their discomfort also, as the reason you are in their life is because they are familiar with your behaviours and the way you react to events. They too are being asked to accept you despite you behaving in a rather unfamiliar way. This leads to discomfort, especially if they too have a great deal yet to learn, and we often find that the responses of friends are what drive people to limit their responses to the opportunity being presented to them, which is somewhat unfortunate. I am hopeful that, armed with this knowledge, you will feel it necessary to continue responding differently.

It is important to respond in different ways each time in the hope of learning.

How to respond in different ways

Each of you is now armed with the knowledge that when scenarios are presented to you it is necessary to have a different response each time, and I have a suggestion for how to do that. I would like you to become more aware of when these situations are being presented as they are not always so extreme. All that is required to recognise a learning challenge is a sense of *Oh, this is happening again.* It is often accompanied by a desire to remove yourself from a particular situation as it is likely this has been presented to you many times before, and there is reluctance on your part to step forward and put yourself in an uncomfortable position. However, that is exactly what you need to do in order to achieve your learning. I am hopeful that, now you are in a position where you are able to understand the reasons for this situation being presented to you, you will feel a little less reluctant to embrace what is about to happen. It would be particularly good if you were able to consider your typical responses in the past and respond on this occasion in a different way. It is important this step is undertaken because, as we have said before, it is only after learning has occurred that these scenarios will stop being presented to you. After this period of learning you are in a position to relax for a while before the next scenario presents itself, and providing the learning has occurred the subsequent scenario will be for a different lesson.

There are a great many of you who, in your frustration at being unable to learn particular lessons throughout a number of lives, line up a considerable number of lessons in this life. This means that, having learned one lesson, it is necessary to move on fairly promptly to the next in the hope of achieving everything you hoped to achieve, and we are hopeful this will help many of you understand the reason why some people have such difficult lives. It is unfortunate as life is not particularly comfortable when so much learning is undertaken; however, there are those who return to us full of joy and pleasure at having achieved much of what they set out to achieve. There are also, however, many who do not achieve so much and instead choose to avoid many of the scenarios that are presented to them, and this is rather unfortunate as it means another life will need to be attempted. I am aware for many of you there is a great deal of discomfort at the learning that is presented to you, but I would like to ask you all to be as brave as you can and appreciate this is very much your choice. I hope that, armed with that knowledge, you will feel somewhat braver in responding in a different way the next time a particular scenario presents itself to you.

I am aware I have covered much of this information previously but I would now like to add something more. It is important each of you is aware of your reasons for being there, and they are, as we have said, to learn, grow and enjoy yourself, and it is essential you feel able to address these issues. To have a great deal of fun and enjoyment lightens your spirit and allows you to be rather more receptive to scenarios that are presented to you. It is important throughout this period of growth and learning that you are able to enjoy much of your life.

I would like to say how important I think it is for many more of you to focus your energy on making the most of your time, as so many focus all their energy on simply existing on earth. While we appreciate there is a great deal of importance in that, it is also important to make the most of your time in regard to learning what it is you intended to learn, and also to have a great deal of enjoyment. In days of old this was not such an issue as people would often work long, hard hours and then at the end of the week make a point of having a great deal of fun, but this seems to have been abandoned by society today as people are constantly attached to various electrical devices and seem unwilling to enjoy the company of others. This fills us with a great deal of disappointment as it is simply not possible for anyone to learn and grow while attached to these devices. There is far more to be gained by connecting with a friend or neighbour than with a person who is on the other side of the world, as when there are problems in the relationship or within your life, that reflects out to the rest of the world via your personality. When people are connected virtually there is a tendency to simply give up as soon as the going gets a little harder; however, if a person is a personal friend or a neighbour or colleague then it's more likely the situation can be ridden out between you and with a great deal of learning taking place for both parties. So, do you get a feel for how important it is to have more connections that are in person rather than virtual?

There is, however, an element of value to maintaining virtual friendships, in instances where you have perhaps made a connection person to person and it becomes impossible to maintain, e.g. if one of you moves away and a decision is made to maintain that relationship online. In those instances, there is a high level of benefit as a considerable amount of groundwork has already been achieved and the likelihood of maintaining that relationship when either party is struggling is increased; however, if it proves impossible to make a one-to-one connection then it is unlikely that over time the bond between you will be maintained. So, it is always important to do your best to have as many relationships as possible that are face to face, and if this is impossible then try and ensure the virtual relationships are punctuated by occasions where you meet in person. I hope it is clear how important it is to have relationships with each other that are in person.

I would also like to say something about how important it is to try and maintain the relationships you have. It is all too easy to have a disagreement and to make a decision to walk away, and while I appreciate that may indeed be necessary at some point, it is important this is not a response you choose regularly, as it means the relationships you do have will be of insufficient depth and, given that much learning occurs during periods of upset and turmoil, your learning will not take place if the relationship is halted.

It is necessary that many of you place a much higher value on the relationships you have and do your best to maintain them. However, there are times when there is insufficient value in maintaining a particular relationship. It may be that a person has chosen to walk a path that is destructive or unhealthy and their behaviour becomes extremely erratic. While I would urge you to do your best to encourage that person to return to a more acceptable state, there does come a time in some relationships when this is simply not possible and it is necessary to let that relationship go. It is unfortunate but on occasions that is what happens.

I would also like you all to consider how important it is to make a decision about the point at which a relationship is unable to be maintained, given a great deal of learning occurs during times of turmoil and upset. I have a suggestion which I hope will make that decision somewhat easier, and that is when a particular relationship becomes something of a drain on you personally. If you are aware of a sinking feeling in your body when you consider contacting that person, then that is often an indication this relationship has run its course. Each connection a person makes needs to have a degree of pleasure within it, and if a point is reached where you are consistently encountering hardship and difficulty when you contact them then it may be time to let that relationship go. It is important to be aware that this needs to be a regular occurrence; for it to occur once or twice is simply not enough. It may be the individual is struggling particularly hard at that time and able to free themselves; however, if the feeling on your part continues for a considerable time then for your own benefit it may be better to let them go. There comes a time when it is important for people to appreciate their behaviour is unacceptable, and while that may anger them it is hoped they will be able to appreciate that the end of their relationship is due to their own behaviour, thereby giving them an opportunity to do something about it. Unfortunately, when a person is struggling to that extent they are often oblivious to how their behaviour is affecting others; they become somewhat selfish and blame other people for their actions. This is unfortunate; however, it may well be part of their learning and it is not something you need to worry about as the responsibility for their unacceptable behaviour very much lies with the person who is meting out that behaviour, and it is also their responsibility to alter their conduct.

I am hopeful you are all aware of how important it is to accept responsibility for your own behaviour and to appreciate that the behaviour of others is their responsibility. It is not your place to work hard to try and change the behaviour of another as that is entirely down to them. It may be that by offering support you are able to guide them through a particularly difficult patch in their life, but it is not your responsibility to alter how they react to it.

The importance of caring for each other

I would like to say something about how to support an individual who is going through a particularly trying time in their life. All of us will at some point struggle with events that are unfolding before us, and it is important each of you is able to accept help from others when this occurs. Many who find themselves in this situation choose to push people away in order to focus their energies on whatever is being thrown at them; however, there is more to be gained by maintaining these relationships and accepting help and support from those around you. It may be the help offered comes from a person who is not the person you wanted help from, or from an unexpected source, and it is important to appreciate the help which is offered as that particular person may have a great deal of experience of these types of situations, or may simply be the only person who is available at the time to support you. It is on these occasions that we work particularly hard to try and ensure there is some kind of support available to you, and we encourage you all to try and accept the support that is offered as this will make your journey somewhat easier. It is extremely difficult when times are hard to try and bear the weight of that event entirely on your own shoulders, and it is important to have discussions with as many people as possible in order to guide yourself to a successful conclusion.

It may well be as you discuss this situation with others that you become aware the advice being offered is less than helpful; however, even this offers you an opportunity to appreciate that is not a way you wish to go, and allows you to form a clearer picture of the path you wish to take. The situation in question may require a great deal of focus on your part and so it may be necessary to find support from a specialised source, and we encourage you to do exactly that as we believe any form of support is important.

How to exploit opportunities presented to you

Many of you are aware when an opportunity is being presented but instead choose to take an easier path, and while I appreciate not every opportunity is right for you it is nonetheless important that consideration is given in the hope of selecting one that will work well for you. It may be an opportunity works well for the person who is presenting it but will not necessarily work so well for you, so it is important to spend some time weighing up the pros and cons. A great deal of thought should be given to this rather than an instant dismissal as there may well be benefits that are not initially apparent and it is necessary you are able to accept opportunities that allow you to push yourself a little. Your life was not intended to be one easy ride throughout; there will always be opportunities that push you in the hope of encouraging you to learn and grow. It may be if you accept this opportunity you will find at a later date it was not an appropriate one to accept, in which case you are perfectly able to change your mind and alter the decision that was made. I appreciate there are some decisions it's important to accept for a specified period of time, and I am aware there is a greater level of hardship if this proves to not be an appropriate step. It is important in these cases to ensure you have as much input from other people as possible in the hope they are able to shine a light on more of the upsides of your situation. Do not discard this opportunity simply because it will force you to extend yourself; however, it is necessary that a significant amount of consideration is given.

The opportunities that are discarded

It is important to ensure all opportunities are given a great deal of thought, and on the occasions it is decided not to pursue a particular situation it needs to be appreciated that another chance will be presented to you. It may be the next will be a little more beneficial; however, it may also be that your next opportunity is offered to you in the hope you will be willing to step forward and take up the challenge of whatever it is you are choosing to resist learning. It is often the case that there is something you particularly wish to learn and have expressed a desire for that while in spirit, but having incarnated on earth there is an aversion to that particular avenue of learning, and so it is our responsibility to ensure you receive as many opportunities as possible to obtain this learning, and it may be we need to disguise it by presenting it to you in another form. I am aware this makes making a decision somewhat harder for you as it is not possible to know whether the opportunity is simply a waste of your time or whether it is something we have worked hard to find for you and would offer you a greater opportunity to learn and grow. I have a suggestion as to how to be more aware of the direction you need to go in. The next time an opportunity is presented to you I would like you to consider how that decision makes you feel in your body. If there is excitement or anticipation then it is likely this is an opportunity not to be missed; however, if you feel negative in some way then this opportunity is not likely to be the one for you. It may, however, be that you are experiencing both, and if this is the case then it's necessary to spend some time considering what you feel the negative points of that opportunity are, as it may well be the negativity you are feeling is down to fear. I hope that is clear and it is possible to understand the difference between a genuine disadvantage and resistance due to fear, as you may find yourself avoiding a particular situation due to fears that are limiting your development. Alternatively, these concerns may require a great deal of consideration as they have merit, and for your own safety and benefit this is an opportunity that needs to be walked away from. There are times when your fears need to be acted upon, and times when they are all in your head and will limit your life.

When a person has a strong belief in themselves and is fully aware of the importance of their own life it is likely they will be rather more aware of the difference between these types of fears. However, there are those amongst you who have more development that needs to occur and I am aware it is considerably harder for you to differentiate between them. It is important to avoid any situation that threatens your personal safety or where there is insufficient data in this regard. It would be hugely disappointing if an opportunity was turned down simply because the person offering it was perhaps intimidating or offhand; however, in instances like that there is a good opportunity for learning to occur as it will then be important to put in place certain behaviours so you are able to accommodate these rather extreme forms of behaviour.

I will try one more time to describe the difference between these two scenarios. It may be an opportunity is being presented that offers something that appeals to you, but comes with the possibility that you will find yourself in situations where you will be very much alone and unsupported. In this case, unless you are able to provide a level of support, it may be better not to take that opportunity as the need to protect and care for yourself is greater than the need for the opportunity. However, if you find yourself being presented with a similar opportunity but one that fills you with dread or fear, then it may be that although you feel unsupported it does not have within it any threat to your personal safety, in which case it may be something to consider. I'm not entirely sure I have made that any clearer. I am simply trying to offer examples of where it's possible to distinguish between fear of a situation and a threat to your personal safety. I am of the belief that as people develop and grow, this differentiation becomes considerably clearer as they will place greater importance on their own safety and value and anything that threatens it is discarded. I appreciate that for those of you who have rather more development yet to do this is a harder decision to make; however, if you are placed in a position where your personal safety is threatened then it is important to step away as it is not acceptable for anybody to be placed in a situation where their safety is threatened regardless of whether a contract has been signed or an undertaking has been agreed. I hope I have made myself clear.

Embracing opportunities or an easy life?

Some of you are offered a great many opportunities but, due to your desire for an easy life, choose to ignore them. I would like to emphasise that not one of you has chosen to incarnate on earth in the hope of having an easy life, and you are fooling yourself if you think there is anything to be gained from this as you will simply return to spirit full of disappointment and upset. It may be part of your learning to become more involved in this world and take your place in it instead of working to ignore all that is going on around you with the aim of having an easy life. It may be that some people have already learned the lessons they intended to learn, in which case their lives will ease considerably; having said that, there will always be events in people's lives that feel uncomfortable. It is simply impossible to avoid a level of discomfort in your relationships with people on earth.

Even those of you who find relationships too difficult and have chosen to become rather reclusive will return to spirit filled with disappointment and upset at having chosen not to learn any of your lessons.

So, the best advice I can give you all is to get stuck in and learn what you intended to learn, embrace every relationship you can in the hope that there is learning within it, and enjoy yourself along the way.

The importance of valuing yourself

Those of you who are further along in your journey will find you value yourself more. However, for those who are at an earlier stage in your journey, it may be this value has yet to be appreciated, and so I think it's important I say something about the need to learn the value of you.

Everybody on this earth is of equal value to everybody else. There is not one person who has any greater or lesser value than anyone else, and it is important to always remember that. Those who choose to advise everybody else of just how important they are invariably do this because they come from a place where they believe *they* have insufficient value and it is important for them to try and achieve it. They find themselves needing to tell others of the value they have because they are unable to feel that value within themselves. Those of you who are aware of your own value have little need to advise anyone else on theirs as you are secure in the knowledge you already have value.

So, how is it possible to achieve value in yourself? Having appreciated that everybody on earth is equal, it is important to give your needs priority in your life in order to maintain that value. The way to do that is to ensure you are in a position to care for yourself, to not put yourself in situations where you are threatened, and to do things for yourself that you appreciate. It may be you particularly enjoy painting, and in order to value yourself it is important to find time to paint, or it may be that spending time with your family is important to you and so it is necessary to find time to enjoy their company. Do you see? It is important to give yourself the things that give you pleasure to demonstrate to yourself how much you value yourself.

It is also important to look at how you treat yourself, as there are those who choose to participate in rather destructive behaviours, and while it may be these behaviours bring you some pleasure, they are nonetheless still destructive. It is necessary they are either eliminated from your life or a much lesser value is placed on them. The types of things I am speaking of here are habits like excessive drinking, smoking or gambling. While each of these is acceptable in moderation, when they begin to cause destruction or upset it is important to take stock and understand the reasons why you choose to participate in this behaviour. It is likely those who choose to participate excessively in destructive behaviour are reinforcing their belief that they as an individual have very little value. I understand you may believe you are doing something for yourself that you enjoy, but it is important to note you are doing it in a destructive way and it therefore becomes necessary to understand the reasons why, especially as such habits often have an alienating effect on the people who care for you the most. It is very hard to care a great deal for someone who chooses to participate in behaviours that cause them harm.

So, for those of you who do have such habits, I would like to encourage you to sit quietly with yourself and try and understand your reasons. It may be you feel completely overwhelmed by a situation or memories, in which case it may be necessary to find some help in the form of a counsellor or psychotherapist who is able to guide you in understanding the events that have brought you to this point. I am aware there are a great many of you who have less-than-ideal lives; however, I would like to offer encouragement, as understanding the reasons why these events have been presented to you often leads to a great deal of learning. I appreciate for some that may be hard to accept; however, I would like to encourage you to step forward and embrace this opportunity to understand the reasons why you are where you are in your life, and what it is that encourages you to continue in this destructive behaviour. I very much hope you will be able to give yourself this opportunity to learn and grow.

I realise this is not easy and it is likely greater hardship may need to be experienced before it is possible to release yourself from this behaviour, but I cannot encourage you enough to step forward and embrace the opportunity to learn and grow, and to release yourself from the need to abuse yourself in ways that are destructive to you and your health. It is important this opportunity is offered to yourself by yourself, as you have as much value as everybody else and it is vital you are able to appreciate that regardless of whatever it is that has caused you to believe otherwise. Every event a person participates in is an opportunity to learn and grow, and while some may have an enormous effect on your life due to the severity of their conditions, there is nonetheless a great deal of learning for you to obtain from them. I say that in the hope you are able to understand there are a number of positive aspects that can be obtained from situations which for many are too painful to examine. Sometimes examination is exactly what is needed in order to release yourself from the need to destroy yourself with unhealthy behaviours.

I am hopeful that in the future many of you will be able to understand the need for appreciating yourself, and to do your best to accept as many of the opportunities presented to you as possible.

Making the most of interests presented to you

It is important when an opportunity is presented to you that it is accepted as an opportunity to learn and grow. We have previously covered the considerations it is helpful to work your way through before accepting an opportunity, and I would like to offer additional information about the benefits of accepting these challenges. As we have said before, each of you who incarnates on earth has put in a considerable number of requests for what you wish to achieve. Many of these are in regard to your growth and learning; however, many also make requests for other skills you wish to develop, as often these skills are transferable to your life in spirit and offer an extra dimension to a skill you have a desire to use while you are in spirit. These may range from artistic skills to music or to something of a more academic nature. So when you are aware of an interest that appeals to you, it is often your guides working to try and encourage you to pursue that interest. Some of you may be able to combine this interest with your work, but that is not always the case and many choose to acquire these additional skills as a hobby or interest outside of work. It is essential these skills have the opportunity to flourish or at least develop as this gives a great deal of satisfaction on your return home.

For those who are on their last journey on earth, unless we have a strong desire to learn a particular skill, it is unlikely that will be enough to bring us back to an earthly life. So for many this may well be the last opportunity you have to acquire this particular skill, and I say that in the hope of offering you an additional incentive to enjoy certain aspects of your life.

As much time as possible needs to be dedicated to acquiring this skill, though I appreciate that for many, time may not be available until later in life. I appreciate that for those with young families and work to do it is often difficult to find time to pursue a skill or interest that appeals, though for some this skill may be particularly strong, in which case time will be found. I would like you to consider any skill you have a desire to learn and to do your best to find some time in order to develop and refine that skill. You will also find this offers a higher level of enjoyment, and many of the benefits that are achieved through that enjoyment will be reaped while working to develop this skill. So you see not only will you benefit from achieving a particular skill you wish to use on your return to spirit, but there are also benefits to be obtained by enjoying yourself on earth.

It is important to give yourself the opportunity to develop skills that you are interested in, and it may be that your interest lies in learning something you are not quite able to understand. So you may have a sense that you wish to know something about a particular subject but after exploring it realise it was not quite what you wanted. However, you now have a desire to learn something else, and I encourage you to follow those interests. You may well find there is a need to gain a greater understanding in a number of subjects and this may eventually develop into a particular avenue of investigation, or it may simply be you have a desire to have more information on a great many subjects. Each of you needs to pursue any desire you have to collect or develop further skills or knowledge for the betterment of your life both on earth and in spirit.

How to spend more of your time pursuing these interests

I am aware there are many who have extremely busy lives and it is particularly difficult to find time to pursue new skills. However, in the fullness of your life it is hoped there will come a time when there is time available and it's possible to pursue these interests. There are, however, others who simply need a little more discipline to pursue their interests, and to those of you I would like to encourage you to perhaps place a note in your diary in the hope of making an appointment with yourself to pursue a particular interest. Many of you express a desire to participate in a particular type of learning and then find yourself overwhelmed with other things that somehow seem more important, and that which you have a desire to develop gets put to the back of the queue. I am hopeful that by putting a note in your diary it will bring it further up the queue of importance. It may of course be there are simply too many other jobs that need to be achieved; however, I would like to encourage you to continue working on this skill or knowledge you have a desire to develop.

It is also necessary to look at the list of jobs that prevent you from pursuing this aim, as I suspect many are not as important as you initially believed them to be. Many people seem to have a desire to complete unnecessary chores, and as a result this diminishes time available for that which you have a desire to learn. It is somewhat unfortunate; however, I have covered this in a previous chapter and have no great wish to expand on it now. It is necessary a greater importance is given to the things you desire to do as this not only feeds your enjoyment, but also allows you the pleasure of being able to advance in a skill or knowledge you have a deep desire to achieve. Many of you will, I feel sure, have pursued this skill at different points in your life and perhaps been a little disappointed, or feel somewhat thwarted by events and have found a need to put this desire on a shelf to be taken out later, and I would like to encourage those of you who are in that position to do exactly that: to try and find the time to remove it from your shelf and further your interests. It is important for the development of your soul that these interests are pursued at some point in your life as there is a level of disappointment on a person's return home when they realise they were either too busy or filled their time with needless tasks and their desire to learn was lost.

So, I hope that offers you greater encouragement to pursue your interests in whatever form they present to you. I would, however, remind you of the importance that whatever you wish to pursue has no detrimental effect on anybody or anything in your world. It needs to be something that pleases you and yet causes no harm.

How to further develop these skills

Many of you will by now be aware of the need to enjoy yourself while you are on earth, and I am hopeful you will be implementing that need if enjoyment was lacking in your life. However, I would like to add another reason I think it is important to pursue your desire to enjoy yourself, and that is to obtain a level of satisfaction and achievement. It is all very well having a list of jobs you feel the need to complete, but satisfaction is considerably less than that which is achieved by doing things you enjoy. I would like to encourage you to spend more time pursuing your desires rather than a list of jobs, and I am hopeful many of you will be able to give more thought to what it is that drives you to place these jobs above your desire to enjoy yourself. While I appreciate there are chores that need to be accomplished in and around the home, I suggest that many of these can be achieved at a later date; and by that I mean, does your home really need to look like it came out of *Good Housekeeping* magazine, or your garden to look quite so spectacular? It may be if you are able to reduce the amount of time you spend on these projects it will offer you a greater freedom to explore other interests and desires, although your garden may indeed be one of those desires. It is important you are able to pursue other lines of enjoyment and pleasure and be less concerned with your list of jobs.

The need each of you seems to have regarding earning a great deal of money

Many people on earth are consumed with the need to have as much money as it's possible for them to amass, and I would like to challenge that need. I am aware for some there is a belief that it is not possible to have enough money and many spend vast amounts of their time working to increase the amount they have; however, a side effect of this is that a part of you is ignored or repressed, and that is the part of you that needs to spend time enjoying yourself. As a result of this pursuit of money and working overtime to achieve it, there is often an overwhelming need to relax, and so people tend to go out and spend a great deal of money in the pursuit of that. And so while it may be that you are indeed earning more money than you previously did, you are also spending more in the pursuit of relaxation and fun.

Those of you who are caught in this cycle of overworking and spending too much on relaxing need to look at your life and perhaps consider the possibility that if you were to work a little less and put less priority on the need for money, you would in fact have more time in which to enjoy yourself and be able to improve your work-life balance, which I am aware is something of a catchphrase these days. It is extremely important this balance is maintained as when this is not the case there tends to be a great deal more money spent in the pursuit of enjoyment; in these instances, the quality of enjoyment is less and as a result more enjoyment needs to be obtained, and at the end of the month they find they are not so much better off. Do you see the cycle developing here? If a person is able to achieve a better life balance the need to spend so much money in the pursuit of pleasure diminishes, and although their income is a little lower they do not have such a desire to spend money enjoying themselves and so in fact they have more money at the end of the month. I would like to offer this to you all as something to consider as the work-life balance is something that is extremely important to each of you, and something I will say more about later.

13 Appreciation

This subject is rather dear to my heart as it was something I struggled a great deal with when I was on earth. I am hopeful the information I am able to give you will make this part of your life somewhat easier, and that is the importance of maintaining a high level of appreciation for all the wondrous things you have in your life. I have touched on this subject already; however, I would like to say rather more.

Appreciation is something each of you needs to hold dear as it is the major component that enables you to have an easier journey on earth. It costs nothing, requires remarkably little effort and offers enormous benefits to everybody who is able to embrace it. Yet so many choose to look at all the hardships and negatives within your life, and frankly there is no need as each of you has a great deal to be thankful for. Even for those who are struggling to make ends meet, or who have such devastating injuries that you wonder how you can ever function again, appreciation is something that can easily be incorporated into your life. To be able to experience the joys and wonders of your world is something all of you would do well to try and cultivate, as not only does it lighten your energy and make your time on earth somewhat easier, it helps to encourage a sense of gratefulness.

It is curious so many of you seem to find pleasure in the negative aspects of being on earth, as this serves no useful purpose to you or anyone else; in fact it can often make your energy heavier, which means others may find it harder to be in your company as it has a remarkably depressive effect on you and those around you. So if you have a desire to enjoy the company of other people, it is important to be responsible enough to address this need and do your best to appreciate all that life has to offer. I would like it very much if those of you who are guilty of negativity would pay special attention to what I have to say, as this has the potential to alter your life considerably, and I am hoping even those who are able to appreciate life will be able to extend your appreciation in a number of other ways.

For those who struggle to be positive, I would appreciate it if you were able to remember you are on this earth to learn, grow and have a great deal of fun, and that is simply not possible when your energy is heavy and negative. It is necessary to do your best to maintain a higher vibration in the hope of attracting others to learn from, and to grow and have fun with. It is also important to remember how necessary it is to spend time in the company of others as it is simply not possible to achieve these ends without other people. I am aware there are some who struggle a great deal with lifting your energy, but this is something that needs to be pursued and practised. Perhaps if you were to introduce a daily routine of appreciating certain items that surround you – though for some of you this may be a difficult task to achieve. However, I think for the majority it should not be so difficult. I would like to encourage a daily practice of appreciation, to spend a little of your time as early in the day as possible observing the joys of your world, and I believe it will be possible to embrace all your world has to offer and, with luck, this will elevate your energy sufficiently to last throughout the day. It may be that a little more effort is required on your part over a period of time, which I do not believe will be so long, for you to elevate your energy as you learn to appreciate all the wondrous things around you. Even those whose lives are extremely difficult have a great many things to appreciate, and there are, in fact, no exceptions to being able to acknowledge and appreciate all the magnificent things that surround you.

Another way to learn to appreciate things is to observe the fabric of creation. Spend time pondering the developments that have occurred within all forms of life on earth and how remarkably efficient each of these life forms is in being able to survive and procreate, and participate in such a wondrous circle of life. Even rather irritating flies are something to behold when you consider the complexity of what they are able to achieve in order to survive, and how all they do works so beautifully with other forms of life. Everything in this world has a function to perform, and for the most part all forms of life pursue this function efficiently and without complaint – unless of course you are a member of the human race, in which case there is often a great deal of complaint.

To be able to appreciate how your world has evolved and continues to evolve is the beginning of learning to appreciate a great deal more. It is important for all of you to be able to experience the sense that so many people have walked this earth before you. I would like it if you were able to focus your attention on life in all its forms and how it's been able to develop since the beginning of time. I appreciate for the most part we have had a great deal to do with this development, but nonetheless I would like it if you were all able to consider many of the developments that have occurred on your planet to a point where it has been possible for you to walk this earth. Millions of years of evolution have needed to take place in order for your world to look the way it currently does, and while you may feel parts of it are remarkably ugly, they have nonetheless become that way due to many years of development. So it may be worth considering that if you find an area less than pleasant it is simply where it is at the moment; in the future it is likely this will alter and return to its natural beauty. It is also important to have an understanding that all life on earth is precious and needs greater appreciation.

I have previously suggested that each morning on waking you consider a few things you feel able to appreciate, and I am hoping with this technique it will be possible to focus your energy on appreciating all your world has to offer. It may take a few days, but that is not so long. I do have another suggestion which I think may help some of you to develop this skill, and that is to consider the years of evolution that have gone into creating a particular thing. By doing this you will be provided with the ability to look at the world from a different viewpoint and, I think, to become more aware of the kindness of others. The feelings of appreciation that these two practices are able to elicit are somewhat similar, and something I hope each of you will be able to develop.

There are many of you who are working hard to try and cope with life, and in pursuing this struggle to live a good life are unable to observe so many things other people do for you. It would be highly beneficial if you were able to notice the progress you are making, as by developing the ability to observe the kind offerings of others, your journey becomes somewhat easier. Many of you believe you are the only one struggling in this world, and that is simply not the case. By developing this technique, it makes it somewhat easier to acknowledge the kindness of others and provides an opportunity to lift you up and out of what is often a rather gloomy state. Do you see how such little effort can create monumental results?

How to cultivate as much appreciation as you possibly can

I have spoken about the importance of acknowledging the kindness of others and I would now like to try and take that a step further by encouraging you to offer your kindness to other people. It is all very well for those who are struggling in this world to steadily become aware of the kindness of other people; however, it is important you are able to try and join this development. Your world would be a much easier place if all of you were able to offer a greater level of kindness to each other; but it is important each of you is able to acknowledge the kindness that is offered to you first. I am particularly hopeful it will be possible to adopt this technique as it makes the lives of many considerably easier.

As you try and offer your kindness to others, do your best to appreciate that other people are struggling with their lives, and the kindness you offer will lighten the load for them. Remember, like attracts like, and so it is hoped, as you offer greater levels of kindness to other people, it becomes something of a magnet and you are then able to attract greater levels of kindness from others. It may be that more appreciation is required on your part before you are truly able to appreciate the amount of kindness others are offering to you, but it is important to start somewhere. I would, however, place a qualifier on this as I think it's important to ensure the kindnesses you are offering do not allow you to be taken advantage of. It is essential to be aware that it is not acceptable for other people to take advantage and abuse your kindness. If this is the case, step forward, speak your truth and advise the offender of the error of their ways. Please never feel that offering kindness to another person is an invitation for others to take advantage of you as that is simply not the case at all. It may be the perpetrator struggles themselves with accepting kindness from others; however, that is their struggle and not one you need to involve yourself with. It is, however, important you are able to acknowledge their misunderstanding and advise them that taking advantage of you is not an acceptable way for them to behave.

The importance of trying to appreciate the struggles of others

It may well be apparent to you that another person is struggling a great deal with their life while yours is cruising along at a very pleasant pace. It may be you have a desire to ease that person's struggle, and I would like to make a suggestion about how that is possible as I think it is all too easy for someone to step forward and limit the amount of learning a person is able to achieve, albeit with the very best of intentions. I think it would be a good idea if you were to acknowledge to yourself that the person in question is indeed struggling, and it would be a kindness if you were able to acknowledge that struggle to the person themselves as they may well appreciate an offer of support. Perhaps make a suggestion to ease their load, or simply offer them a little of your time. If they rebuff your offering, then so be it; it is not appropriate to take matters into your own hands and force them to accept your kindness. Neither is it appropriate to become upset by the rebuff as it is important to appreciate that not everybody is in a position to accept kindness or time from other people. It may well be that part of their learning is to appreciate the kindness of others, and for now they are simply unable to accept what others are willing to do for them. It may simply be that they are not in a position to accept any kindness from you for any number of reasons, and it is important to appreciate that. It is additionally important that this lack of acceptance is not taken on board by you as a demonstration of how someone feels about you. It needs to be accepted they are unable for whatever reason to accept your kind offer at that particular time and that is all they are saying; no part of this should be taken as any kind of slight directed towards you. Do you see? Simply because a person offers kindness to another person does not mean they must accept it, and if they choose not to accept it is in no way a reflection on you; it is simply that they are unable to accept that kindness for a reason you are not party to. I hope that is clear as I have no wish for any of you to feel hurt by another person's lack of acceptance.

How to find ways to be kinder to yourself

This is something a great many of you struggle with, as we hear so many of you being really unkind to yourselves, and it is significantly easier to be kinder to others if you are kinder to yourself first. It would be good if you were able to hear the kind of things you say to yourself about yourself, as this would give you a good idea of what it is I am trying to focus your attention on. Many of you spend a great deal of time being remarkably hard on yourselves and there is simply no need as all that does is encourage you to have a less-than-kind opinion of yourself. We in spirit are all very aware of how hard life is on earth and there is no need for any of you to make it any harder. It is important to have a far greater appreciation of what you have achieved in this life, which is a great deal. Each of you has so many chores it is necessary to concern yourself with, and many of you try to add more to the list which are completely unnecessary. This adds to the hardships within your life, and continually trying to achieve them makes your life even harder. When it is not possible to meet them you are extremely hard on yourself, and that is something we would like you to try and stop immediately. Putting excessive responsibilities on yourself and then giving yourself a hard time for not completing them is a waste of time and effort. Far better would be to complete what is absolutely necessary, and achieve that, than to give yourself an impossible list and then berate yourself when it is not completed.

It is important a far greater level of kindness is offered to each of you by each of you, and by that I mean the next time you look in the mirror I would like you to say something kind to yourself instead of observing all you believe is lacking, as that is simply not the case; and to acknowledge where you have done your best and appreciate that was all you were able to do. By doing this it becomes considerably easier to observe the kindness of others. It is extremely difficult to be aware of that kindness when you are unable to be kind to yourself. So, I would like it if you were to ease up on yourself and show yourself a much greater appreciation and kindness, as you are all wondrous beings who deserve a far greater level of admiration and appreciation for how well you are doing on your journey on earth. This is not something we particularly struggle with in spirit as we are all very able to appreciate the kindness of others and indeed of ourselves; it is very much a struggle those of you on earth have. So I would like to suggest to you all that you work to make a habit of being significantly kinder to yourself.

How to appreciate all the wonders of your world

It may seem I have covered this but there is something else I wish to add, and that is how important it is for more of you to increase the amount of time you spend appreciating the wonders of your world. It is all very well to have an understanding of the beauty of your world and to stand in nature and be aware of all the life that surrounds you; however, I think it is also important for you to do that with each other as there is a great deal to be gained by appreciating the wonders of the human race. I readily accept for many of you the human race is really rather odd, with everybody's unique way of dealing with situations which can often seem rather strange; however, I would like to point out how wondrous that uniqueness is and how many different permutations there are to each situation.

It may be you see an event in a particular way and to you there is only one way to respond to that event; however, to others there are different ways that make perfect sense to them, and I appreciate for some that is difficult to accept. However, you are all unique and that means your responses to particular situations will also be unique, and it is important to appreciate that. I accept wholeheartedly that if there are a number of you in a particular situation and a response is required and each person chooses a different response then the situation can get quite heated, and I would like to offer a suggestion as to how that can be resolved.

Each person's opinion on how to react needs to be respected and I suggest that first you listen to everybody's ideas and then offer an unbiased and appropriate solution. It is important not to choose your own solution simply because it's yours, but to be open enough to appreciate that often other people have ideas you simply have no concept of, and so a solution can be found in their suggestions too. It may be there are those amongst you who feel their solution was the best. If so, it is important to try and appreciate the other person's solution but also explain to them the reason you have chosen another. You also need to be honest with yourself as to the reason you have chosen a particular course of action, as simply selecting one because you like the person who suggested it and wish to court favour with them is not a suitable reason. It is necessary you are able to be as unbiased as possible and select the option that works best for not only the situation, but everybody who is present and will be affected by the outcome. It is essential to consider the greater good rather than your favourite solution. That way, in the future, if anybody is upset about what was chosen you are able to explain to them clearly and truthfully the reason you chose that route.

It may be that in the fullness of time that route proves to be less than beneficial as circumstances change; however, this allows you then to say that given the circumstances at the time, you selected the solution that worked best for everybody rather than just a few, or even just yourself. Do you see the point I am trying to make: how important it is to consider the situation and the outcome of your decision and to ensure the selected outcome is not necessarily your own?

How to appreciate the opinions of others

There are times when you bump into people who have a great many opinions which they seem determined to share; this is unfortunate as, for the most part, it is unnecessary. I would like to highlight a solution to this. Firstly, it is important to listen to their opinions, at least to begin with, as it may become a little overwhelming to be with someone who has so many opinions; then to appreciate the reason they have so many opinions, and there are a number of reasons why this may be the case. The main reason, I believe, is because no one has spent much time listening to their solutions on any given subject and in their frustration at feeling so insignificant they do their best to ensure that situation doesn't happen again, and as a consequence they are rather free and easy with their opinions. It may be, however, that they developed this technique as they were amongst rather ineffectual people and it became important for somebody to step forward and take charge, and that is what they chose to do, in which case they have become rather used to their opinions being considered important.

I believe these are the two main reasons people find themselves being rather opinionated on many subjects; however, I am sure there are a number of other reasons that people have become this way and it is important for you to appreciate that they have done so for very good reasons.

I would now like you to consider the importance of these people being given a free rein to express their opinion on a particular subject; however, it is essential everyone else is also afforded that opportunity, and for you to appreciate that everybody's opinion is equally important. I appreciate when making a decision it can be somewhat easier to select the opinion of the person who is being rather more forthright in their desire to command the situation; however, you need to maintain a level of strength in this regard and select the option you feel is the best, and to be able to offer this solution in an unbiased and clear way to those who will be affected. It is necessary you are able to hold your ground and ensure that the solution you have selected has been chosen because it is the best solution rather than simply one that will calm the people who are involved. I am aware for many this is not easy as some people can have quite dominant personalities and believe their opinions are the ones to listen to, and it is important to ensure the solution you have selected is the best for that particular situation and not necessarily the best for the people within it.

Learning to speak your mind

As I have tried to explain throughout this book, it is essential to do your best to listen to your body as it reacts to situations, as this is often the strongest way to ensure you are responding genuinely. When an opportunity is offered that your body indicates may be positive then it is imperative you are able to step forward and take up that challenge. It may be that those around you do not see this offer as something that would benefit you; however, if your body is indicating this is the case it is important you take up that particular challenge, and when you do you will be safe in the knowledge that it is very much something you wished to take on board. If in the future it turns out that this opportunity was perhaps not the most beneficial then you will always know that you chose the best outcome given the circumstances you were in at the time. It is essential all of you are able to appreciate this, as each of you is unique in your requirements for this life, and while something may seem to be totally wrong for one person that does not necessarily mean it is the case for everybody, and it is important to consider that in order to select the best option.

You need to feel able to stand by the decision you have made, sometimes despite great opposition from other people, confident that you have chosen the response that works best for you, as there are many people who feel their response to a given situation is the one that everybody else should take. However, that is not always the case and it is important to learn to appreciate how unique each of you is and to maintain that uniqueness throughout your life. It is likely some will struggle with this; however, that is part of their learning as none of you is there to live the lives of other people.

I would also like to say how valuable it is for each of you to become accustomed to steering your own way through the challenges presented to you while on earth. It is necessary to feel satisfied you are choosing these particular options because they are the ones that work best for you at that particular time, and only you are able to make that decision. Do you see how important it is to stand up for yourself when decisions are made that others disagree with? I hope over time those of you who struggle with this concept will be able to develop ways that work for you.

Each of you needs to follow your own path, as your world has a great many wondrous things to offer; however, it is different for each of you and it is important you are able to appreciate that, as somebody else's perfect life will never be your own.

How to become more aware of your own needs

We have discussed the importance of listening to your body and observing solutions to situations you are placed in; however, there are occasions when it is paramount to listen to the advice of your head, although your head and the information processed within it do not necessarily work for your best interest. Often that information is very much based on facts and data and does not necessarily have the interests of you as an individual at heart, though I do appreciate that will not always be the case. So, it is important when deciding on a particular course of action to weigh up the pros and cons and do your best to get as much information as possible. It may be you require more information from a person who is a specialist in a particular area, or it may be a good idea to discuss the matter with friends in order to get a few more opinions. Whatever you choose to do, it is vital to get some excellent input into how to make the best decision. It may be an idea to list the strengths and weaknesses of the situation, or to select one particular option and run with it, although I am not sure that is necessarily the best way to resolve a situation. It is helpful to consider possible outcomes, and it is my hope that, over time, while processing this decision, you will find yourself drawn to a particular course of action, and as you feel drawn to that, it is beneficial to understand your reasons. It may be you have a better picture of the solution that needs to be taken up, or it may be you find yourself trying to talk your way out of a particular situation, and while this may be an excellent way to resolve the opportunity that has been presented to you it may also be a way to avoid embracing an opportunity that is an excellent idea. So, please be honest with yourself about why you are choosing to respond in a particular way.

I would like it if more of you were able to be more honest with yourselves and to respond more positively. It is all very well knowing you have been presented with an excellent opportunity and have talked yourself out of it through fear; however, that opportunity is still missed, which is not a particularly good idea as many people have gone to a great deal of trouble to ensure an opportunity that was good for you was presented to you. So, despite your reservations it would be far better to embrace the opportunity. I hope that is clear.

How to recognise situations offered to you

I think for many of you it is paramount to be aware of when an opportunity is being presented, and there are a number of ways you will be able to do that. The first is obvious, when an opportunity is clearly presented and it is necessary to make a decision; and I think for the most part I have covered what is necessary to help make that decision. I do think, however, one way to become aware of an opportunity being presented is as soon as a decision needs to be made in regard to how you wish to live your life. It may be an opportunity is presented that is not particularly big; however, there is something about it that appeals and it is essential you are able to give some time to considering its pros and cons. In going through that process, if it feels as though there is a level of positivity and benefit then it may well be best to pursue that avenue, as I have no wish for any of you to turn down possible opportunities that would benefit your life. When an opportunity is offered that does not work well for your life – although it may work well for other people, possibly the people who are offering it to you – it is important to employ the criteria I have mentioned earlier and not take up that opportunity. As you become more practised at responding to situations it becomes easier, and over time you will be able to feel in your body the types of opportunities that work well, and have more confidence in standing up for yourself and the routes you have chosen to take. It is not the place of anybody else to make that judgement on your life as the life you are living is your own, and it is equally important the decisions you make in your life are for your own benefit and not taken as a response to the reactions of others or with an intention of causing an effect to another person.

14 The Importance of Feeling Grateful

For each of you on earth it is important to develop the ability to feel grateful for the benefits that are offered to you. The reason this is so important is that this too helps to lighten your energy and, along with appreciation, make your time on earth considerably easier. I appreciate there is a fine line that separates appreciation and gratefulness; however, there is without doubt a difference (the former being more concerned with recognition of acts, whereas the latter is more akin to feeling thankful for something that has happened). To hold both within yourself offers you a far greater opportunity to lift your energy, which is extremely beneficial as it is very easy throughout your life on earth to trudge along with a rather heavier energy than you need, and with that weight comes a great many disappointments as your journey becomes more of a struggle than it needs to be. A few simple tweaks are all that's needed for your energy to lift and your time on earth to be considerably easier.

One of the ways to do that is to cultivate a level of gratefulness for all the benefits that are afforded to you, and there are a number of ways to achieve that. One of those is simply to, at the end of your day, say thank you and possibly list all the things you wish to say thank you for. Even those of you who have extremely hard lives with a great deal of struggle have a number of things for which it's possible to feel grateful. It may be due to the worry of the state you are in that has caused an upset with people who are around you. I would, however, like you to consider how much worse the situation could have been and then say thank you for that not being the case, and to perhaps look into other aspects of your day and be able to appreciate that your day could have been considerably worse. Once you have appreciated that, it would be marvellous to say thank you. I say this simply as a way to begin; I have no great wish for you in the long term to consider how much worse your life could have been and I am not sure there is much to be gained by focusing on such negativity. However, I offer that simply as a way to begin your journey of gratefulness.

Another suggestion which I think will help you is to spend a little of your time, and this needs only to be brief, considering the rather wonderful things that have happened in your world and to say thank you for those. There is a growing trend for people to note the wonderful things that can happen to others that reflect the kindness of people. It would be excellent to say thank you for these even though the effects of the event are all that have touched your life; the actual event happened to someone else and it is for them to say thank you also.

Another suggestion is to become rather more aware of the kindness of other people, as each of you has within you a well that holds a great deal of kindness, and when you are in a position to observe the kindness of other people it would be splendid if you were to say thank you. It may help to say it to the person who was offering the kindness; however, if you are rather new to observing the kindnesses of others it may take a little while to appreciate what they have done for you and so if you were to say thank you at some point before your days end that would help. Gradually it will become possible to acknowledge the kindness of others at the time; however, this may take a little practice as I appreciate for many of you life can be a considerable struggle and if you have spent many years battling with that struggle it is often difficult to observe the kindness of others, or perhaps easy to assume the kindness that is offered has an ulterior motive. However, people have a desire to offer kindness to others and while there may be an ulterior motive it would do you well to acknowledge the kindness that surrounds it.

There is another suggestion I would like to make which I think will help you to develop a greater level of gratefulness, and that is to observe the kindness that is offered by governments, entrepreneurs or those with a great deal of wealth, for the benefit of others. There are many people and governments who are willing to try and lift the lives of others; however, considerable numbers of you have a great deal of cynicism regarding this kind of behaviour, which is really rather unfortunate as the benefits to many people are truly enormous and it would be a great kindness if you were to say thank you. It may seem that to say thank you for something others have done in distant lands will have no impact on you at all; however, it is important to become more aware and to say thank you for all the goodness and kindness that is in your world as there is in fact a great deal. It is unfortunate so much news is focused on the negative aspects of your world, and as a result that tends to be what people see, yet that is not the whole story; there are a great many very positive stories that could be mentioned, and news items that have been slanted to appear negative as the producers believe negative news is more popular. However, if you were to look at a particular situation from a different viewpoint you will be able to notice there is a great deal to be grateful for. Do you see how different a situation can present if you simply look at it from a different viewpoint and appreciate the kindness of others by saying thank you?

Not only does this help develop your own gratefulness, but simply by acknowledging the goodness of other people there is a lift in the energy of your world, and that is something we would like to encourage. Much of the energy within your world is rather heavy and needs lifting, and once it has lifted, even a little, this will have a highly beneficial effect on the inhabitants of earth. It may seem very small to say thank you for the kindness of others; however, thoughts have energy and any way it's possible to think something positive and put it out into the world will have as much effect as someone who chooses to send a negative thought out into the world, and we are hopeful over time more and more of you will work with positive thought and gradually the negativity will diminish. We appreciate this will take a great many years; however, it is important as many people as possible are able to take on board the need for lifting the energy in your world to try and make that world a rather more pleasant place to live in. Do you see? I am very aware many of you will struggle to believe that a simple thank you at the end of the day will make a difference, but in time it will not only be you; it will, we hope, be many thousands doing exactly that, and that *will* have an impact.

I hope in the fullness of time it will be possible for a great many of you to make it a habit to simply say thank you for all the wonderful things that have happened in a particular day; and gradually your world will change.

How important it is to appreciate the kindness of others

I am aware I have mentioned this in a previous chapter; however, I am able to add a little more and I think now would be a good time as this does require a level of gratefulness.

I would like it very much if more of you, having appreciated the kindness of other people, were able to not only acknowledge that kindness, but also try and pass kindness on to others. I hope over time as your sensitivity to the kindness of other people develops it will be possible to feel that kindness instead of simply observing it, and as you are able to feel it, it becomes possible to pass that feeling on to other people by showing kindness to them. This has the effect of lifting not only your own energy, but that of others, as they are then able to appreciate the kindness you have offered them. All of us here in spirit hope that over time this will take on a life of its own and the kindness that each of you is able to offer everybody else will become the norm.

We are aware there are a number of people in your world who work hard to try and highlight the kindness of others and to encourage other people to pass that on, and they deserve a great deal of commendation for their work. Any effort you are able to make would benefit not only those involved but also the energy held within your world, as it adds a great deal of lightness. So, the benefits of being kind, acknowledging the kindness of others and being able to say thank you have far-reaching effects; in fact they have a major effect in changing your world, which is something we believe a great many of you wish to do. Simply by changing your own attitude you are able to do exactly that and help to alter the planet you live on. So gradually, as you are able to acknowledge the kindness of others, pass that on and feel a level of gratefulness; your world will steadily improve as more people are able to acknowledge and offer kindness. I hope it is possible to grasp the truly magnificent effect that simply saying thank you and acknowledging kindness will have on your world.

How important it is to change the energy within your world

There is currently a great deal of war and upheaval going on in your world and this needs to stop. We are aware there are many of you who would like this to stop but feel powerless to do anything about it, and we understand that; however, it is excellent that so many of you are able to appreciate that this situation and the struggles of those caught up in it are unacceptable. These wars are often caused by a great deal of upset and anger in the lives of the perpetrators, and while we appreciate for many it will be extremely difficult to have a level of understanding for this it is nonetheless the way it is. People react to the circumstances given to them and it is important these circumstances are lifted, and we believe if the energy within your world was somewhat lighter then it would be possible for everybody to live easier lives. The way we would like that to begin is for all of you to have appreciation and gratefulness for all the kindnesses in your world. Over time this will spread and even those who are struggling with their lives will be able to grasp the importance of acknowledging the kindness of other people. It is likely this will take many years as there are various enclaves within the world where there is a great deal of bitterness and anger, and in those areas it will take a considerable effort to break down the negativity. Many people who feel such anger and bitterness have placed themselves in rather dangerous positions in order to try and ease the overwhelming feelings they have, and that is something we would like to stop as you are not there to struggle due to the anger and bitterness of others. It is never appropriate for anyone to inflict their beliefs on another person – ever.

Each of you is on earth to live a life of freedom, with opportunities to learn, grow and have a great deal of fun, and it is important every member of society who is able does exactly that. The way we would like you to do this is to have a greater sense of gratefulness and appreciation for all the goodness and kindness that is in your world, and simply by adopting that habit you will find over time your world will change.

There are amongst you people who choose to promote the need to reduce the number of wars by organising peace marches, and while we appreciate the goodness and kindness behind this, we think there would be more benefit if you were to try and promote greater levels of harmony. There is an excellent reason for why we say that: you see, there are certain rules that exist within the universe which cannot be broken; they are simply rules that need to be accepted and lived by, and one of those rules is that wherever there is an event there is always an equal and opposite event that occurs somewhere else in the world. That is an absolute rule and it is simply not possible for it to be broken by anybody, and so it is important to be aware that while the opposite of war is peace, the opposite of peace is war. So while we appreciate many of you are doing your level best to try and improve the lot of others, by going on peace marches you are inadvertently encouraging the continuation of war in other parts of the world. We have no wish for any of you to take this as criticism as we appreciate your efforts come from the kindest of places; however, we would encourage you to alter your stance and perhaps march for harmony, and work towards a place where harmony has a greater impact in your lives. I hope I have made that clear as I am aware there are a great many of you who have a desire for peace and we would like it very much if that desire were replaced by a desire for harmony throughout your world. It is extremely important more of you are able to take up the importance of harmony, as the effects will be profound; the lives of many will change, and very much for the better.

15

How to Stand Up for Yourself

I have a few suggestions about how it's possible for you to be somewhat stronger and able to be the person you hoped to be when you incarnated on earth. Many of you choose to hold a great deal of fear about being yourself and standing up for yourself, and as a consequence life becomes a struggle, but it's important to master this in the hope of living an easier and freer life. There are many ways to develop techniques that enable you to stand up for yourself; however, I think this is the main one that allows your confidence to build gradually.

It is all very well making a decision to become more confident and stand up for yourself more, and for some this does work; however, it is easy to, for whatever reason, get knocked off course as there is no depth to the route you have chosen to take. If each of you choose to stand up for yourself in smaller ways and do that over a period of time you will find that when a situation presents that is less than beneficial you are able to maintain your confidence far easier than if you had simply chosen to make that decision. Do you see how one method has a great deal more depth to it, and the other, being so shallow, is easy to shy away from?

It is important each of you has a strong idea of what is needed as there are so many who find themselves being ignored and walked over and that is not something we would like any of you to continue doing. We additionally have no wish for you to become an opinionated person or someone who would ignore other people's ideas, so I feel it is necessary to try and point out the special place that exists between the two extremes. I am hopeful I will be able to offer you some information on how to find a way to live in that in-between place.

I am of the belief that those of you who struggle to stand up for yourselves do so because of fear that something you say or do may be ridiculed in some way, and it is important to get past that. When you believe this about yourself it becomes easy for others to ridicule you when you offer an explanation or suggestion, simply because it is done in such a way that invites the exact thing you are trying to avoid, and so I would like to offer some suggestions to avoid that.

For those of you who struggle with this, consider how you would feel faced with yourself. Would you feel inclined to ridicule yourself when you offer a suggestion, or would you be kind enough to listen and take it on board? I say that because I think it's necessary to have an understanding of how your behaviour affects other people, and it may be you choose to offer your suggestion in a way that invites ridicule, perhaps because it is offered in a small and insignificant voice, rather than stepping forward and offering your suggestion with the validity you believe it has. I hope you understand the difference there as it is significant to the people who are receiving your suggestion. There are those amongst you who are so full of insignificance and fear that when you do eventually offer a suggestion it comes out in a very tiny voice and it is difficult for those listening to take it seriously, and I am hopeful I can offer a few hints to help you get past those feelings.

For the most part it is important to embrace the idea that everybody is equal and entitled to an opinion. It may be someone's opinion carries a little more weight than others simply because they have more experience and knowledge in a particular situation; however, that is not necessarily the case as often a group of people will be asked for their opinion on a particular topic because there is confusion, and the reason you have been asked is because there is a belief that your opinion is worthy. Do you see? If the person asking the question was not interested in receiving your reply then they would never have asked for it in the first place. So, I hope that gives you a start on the importance of valuing what you have to say, as clearly others do.

It is also necessary to consider that while everybody on earth is equal and every soul is equal, opinions differ in regards to the knowledge people hold; however, in situations where there is no prior specialist knowledge available and no guarantee of what an outcome may be then anybody's opinion has as much validity as anybody else's and it is important to remember that. Your suggestion may not necessarily be the solution that is accepted for a particular situation, and that is fine as it is simply not possible for everybody's solution to be employed. It is also important to remember when you are offering your opinion that it needs to be offered in a way the recipient feels able to take seriously. It is no good making a joke of it or laughing at yourself or anyone else as this means the recipient will struggle to take you seriously. So not only is it important for it to be spoken in a voice that is confident or at least appears confident to those listening, but it is also important not to undermine the information you are willing to offer. You could practise this at home; simply practise offering a suggestion to someone, but do so in a mirror so you are fully aware of how you appear, while trying to be non-judgemental of yourself. Simply observe in as detached a manner as possible and try to understand how someone might feel if you were to offer your suggestion in the way you currently do. That may give you a better feel of what it's like to receive the information you are offering, as it is important to do so with an attitude of equality and full understanding that what you have to say has as much value as what anybody else has to say.

I would now like you to consider how important it is to deliver your message in a way that holds a great deal of value. Not only is it important not to undermine yourself or speak in a rather feeble voice, but it is also important to explain your suggestion in a way that can be taken seriously, and by that I mean using words people will understand. It is no good trying to impress someone else with your opinion and using words that make the understanding of your message somewhat difficult; nor is it acceptable to offer your suggestions couched in foul language as this too will have an undermining effect. The information needs to be delivered in a way that is easily understandable and has no level of aggression within it, which is not what happens when people swear.

I would now like to suggest a way for you to practise this. I think it is crucial each of you practises offering your suggestions to others in order that when the day arrives and you are asked for your opinion it is something you have done a number of times and so you will be prepared and willing to offer a suggestion that is not shrouded in feelings of inadequacy or presented with a great deal of aggression behind it. It should simply be offered with a level of appreciation for its quality. Do you see how different people's suggestions can be? It is important to take yourself seriously in the hope that this will encourage you to deliver a serious suggestion that will be taken on board as a valid option. I hope I have made that clear, as I do believe a great deal of preparation can be done by offering suggestions to yourself in a mirror and trying to understand the points I have made above. You could perhaps practise using the methods I have suggested you *don't* use in the hope of getting a feel for what it is you are trying to avoid. If you choose to employ that idea I would also like to suggest that when you have completed your exercise you repeat a few times how it is you *do* wish to offer your opinion, in order to become more comfortable with it.

Having grasped the need to speak to others offering your opinions it is helpful if ways are developed for speaking clearly and confidently by ensuring that when your opinion is requested you are able to offer it devoid of any kind of emotion, as that was not what your questioner was asking for. It needs to be offered in a dispassionate way, otherwise recipients find they are more aware of the emotion behind a suggestion than they are of the suggestion itself; this can easily taint the information you have offered, and that needs to be avoided at all costs. Each of you needs to be aware of what a suggestion feels like when it is couched in emotion, so again I suggest you practise in a mirror and deliver your message with various emotions behind it, exaggerated in order to have a full idea of what it looks and feels like to wrap a suggestion in emotion. Emotions are something that need to be kept in check and used at specific times. It is not a good idea to allow your emotions to taint information you wish to deliver as you will become aware that people have no wish to be informed of your emotional state when they are seeking information; that is for another time. It is important not to use any opinion you offer as a way of demonstrating your displeasure or any other emotion you may be feeling at the time. If you have a wish to be taken seriously by others you need to take yourself seriously, and to douse any suggestion you have in emotion is clear evidence you are not taking yourself seriously as it is highly inappropriate to offer suggestions to others which are shrouded in your emotions. It is entirely acceptable to have emotional feelings on any number of subjects, but when you are offering an opinion it is not an appropriate time to let them out.

Many of you, I believe, try hard to offer suggestions to others about how their lives could go rather better than they currently do, and while you may have their best interests at heart it is none of your business and highly inappropriate.

Consider how you feel when somebody offers you their opinion about your life and how they think it would run better if you were to employ their ideas. I am sure most of you would feel rather irritated that they believe their ideas are superior to your own, and that is how others feel when you offer your opinion about their lives. It may be you are aware they are doing something rather foolish that they would do well to stop, in which case it is in your interest to ask them if they are willing to hear what you have to say. It may be they have no wish to hear your opinion, in which case it is not your place to offer it; however, if they offer their encouragement then it would be appropriate to offer your opinion. Again, it is important all the above suggestions are employed as it is necessary they are able to hear what you have to say without it being dressed in either aggression or emotion or timidity. Do you see how necessary it is for them to be willing to understand what you are saying without it being clouded in emotion? If you feel it is important to offer a suggestion to another person then it is important it is offered clearly and easily with no hidden agendas.

It may be the recipient of your opinion chooses not to take on board what you are saying and that is fine; they are as able to accept your opinion as they are to choose to ignore it. It is of course their life to do with as they wish and they are very much more aware of their reasons for behaving in a particular way. It may be the suggestion you offered them is not something they are able to take on board at this time, or it may be something they choose to employ at a later date, and so I would like to suggest the importance of accepting the fact that they may choose not to take on board what you have said even though you believe it comes from the kindest of places. I hope it is clear that while you are free to offer your ideas to another, they do not necessarily have to take them up, and it is of course important to only offer those ideas if the other person is willing to listen. It is unacceptable for anyone to provide their opinions on another person's life without first accepting permission, as that is tantamount to bullying and needs to be avoided at all costs. Your opinion holds no more weight than their own about how they choose to live their life. It is never appropriate for somebody to tell another how they should live their life, unless of course they are children and their parents are offering guidance.

The importance of speaking your mind

There is a great deal to be gained if you are able to speak your mind clearly, devoid of any emotion. There are occasions when it is necessary to allow your emotional side to shine through; however, in situations where you are dealing with people, perhaps within a work setting or a setting of conflict, it is necessary to remove the emotion and try to speak as clearly as you possibly can. This will allow you to speak openly and freely, as it is important when you are trying to resolve a situation that you are able to say what is on your mind. The point of the exercise is not to bully the other person into accepting your belief, but simply to state how you feel at that particular time on that particular topic. It may be your recipient has insufficient development themselves to be able to accept the information you are offering, and it is therefore in your best interest to perhaps offer some more information as a response.

So if, for instance, you were able to offer a suggestion to a particular problem and your recipient came back with a great deal of emotion, then I would like you to hear what they have said and respond to that, again devoid of any kind of emotion. It may be necessary to be extremely brave, as if another person is highly emotional it can be rather intimidating; however, I urge you to stand up for yourself and say openly and clearly what is on your mind. It may be your recipient loses all sense of control and becomes overly emotional, in which case there is little to be achieved by continuing the conversation, and it may be necessary to simply walk away and suggest completing your discussion when they have calmed down. It may be you have to remain in that situation to calm them down; however, it is important the discussion is stopped until such time as the other person has calmed. This is something that occurs a great deal in relationships where one person has a desire the other does not, and they are usually underpinned by a level of fear on one or even both sides. It would be beneficial to look at the discussion you are having, to try and determine whether or not that is the case. If it is it may be necessary to voice those fears in order for your recipient to have a better idea of what is going on between you. It may be they have become highly emotional due to their own fears, in which case an admission of your own is often reassuring and allows them the space to open up, and with luck that will allow the situation to alter considerably and for you both to be more open and honest with each other. It may take a period of time to be able to reach that point; however, it is necessary in order to reach a solution. If you are able to work your way through this process it has a better chance of resolution than if you continue trying to solve the issue without fully understanding what is going on. I hope that is clear and offers a greater level of understanding as to how important it is to speak your mind clearly and free of emotion.

I think you all need to consider the importance of the value each of you has for yourself in order to project an air of validity and to feel that within yourself, and I would like to offer some suggestions as to how that is possible.

I am aware many of you have had parents who perhaps were a little undermining of you as you grew up and there may be any number of reasons why that was the case; however, it is necessary to move past that place and appreciate that your opinions are as valid as anybody else's. It is important to be aware of how valuable you are, and to do that by ensuring what it is you have to say on any subject is offered to others in a way that indicates your value. This does not mean shouting or enforcing your opinions; it simply means being free to state what you believe to be true. It also means being free to appreciate that another person's opinion may in fact provide a better solution to an issue than your own, and having the flexibility to take that on board.

I believe the reason each of you feels undermined or that your beliefs hold less value than another's is because that is how you feel inside, but it is simply a belief of yours. It is important you are able to overcome the disadvantage you are giving yourself, as your beliefs and opinions have as much value as anybody else's; it is simply a question of altering your mindset. This does not mean your opinions are any *more* important than anybody else's; it simply means they have as much value, and if you feel at any time that is not the case then it is necessary to spend a little time considering the reason behind that. It may be you were brought up in a rather bullying or aggressive home and as a consequence you were never allowed to have an opinion, or any opinions you had were belittled, in which case you need to remember that was due to the aggression of another person. It was no reflection on you; the reflection you were seeing was that of the bullies. They were the ones who were forcing their opinions on you and others, and that does not mean what they said and did was correct. It is something you need to consider deeply and understand that kind of behaviour is totally inappropriate, and while it was necessary to endure that period in your life it is no longer the case and you now need to move past that feeling. Do you see? I hope that's clear; I appreciate it may take you some time to get past the experience of people forcing their opinions on you but it is something that needs to be learned and developed.

Why standing up for yourself has such a beneficial effect on your life

You will find if you are able to adopt many of the techniques I have mentioned above that your life will progress in an entirely different way, and if you can also accept that not only your opinions but you as a person are as valid as everybody else, you will find your life changes completely. Suddenly you will become aware of how different your world feels. Instead of being a victim of the whims of others you will be able to step forward and take your place in this world, and it is important every one of you is able to do that. I am aware for some this journey will be particularly arduous;

however, it is a journey that needs to be undertaken as it is extremely important every one of you is aware of your own importance. You are all unique and valuable and your opinions count as equally as everybody else's. It may take many years to appreciate that, but it is something each of you needs to pursue. I am aware for many this will require a great deal of bravery and it is likely there will be many attempts on your part to change how you feel about yourself. However, it is important to realise that this is part of your learning and it is necessary to practise the techniques I have suggested above in the hope you are able to advance the learning you are there to achieve.

The importance of being yourself

I think it is important for many more of you to have a better understanding of who you are and the reasons you chose to incarnate on earth. We have covered that you are all there to learn, grow and have a great deal of fun; however, each of you needs to have a thorough understanding of how you are able to make the most of that. It is necessary to spend some time becoming aware of your shortcomings and all the things you struggle with in this life, and that will give you a good idea of the kind of learning you are there to achieve. If you are in the position of being unable to consider anything you struggle with then there may be one of two things happening. It may be you have learned everything you hoped to learn and are therefore in the enviable position of being able to enjoy the rest of your life; on the other hand, it may be you are simply in denial. It is important to establish which of these is the case, as on the one hand you may be denying yourself a great deal of fun, and on the other the life you are leading may be having a considerable impact on those around you and you are oblivious to this. It is necessary to understand this difference as there will be a great deal of disappointment on your return to spirit when you discover there were many opportunities to learn but you were oblivious to each of them; and so I have a suggestion that I think may help in your understanding of which of these categories you belong to.

If you find along life's journey there are a number of occasions when those around you feel extremely frustrated then it may be you are choosing to ignore any opportunities you are offered to learn. On the other hand, if that is not the case then it's likely you have learned all you hoped to learn. There are not so many who are in that position, as for most people there remain smaller lessons to learn; however, such people certainly exist. So, for those who are aware of frustration in other people around you it may be time to take a closer look at the reasons for that as it's likely you are the cause. It may be this frustration is part of their learning; however, there is likely to be a level of learning on your part that is required and it is important to have a thorough understanding of what you believe is going on in these instances. You may be of the belief that the learning required is entirely on the other person's side and you are simply there for them to learn from; however, it may be necessary to have a clear idea of the reason they feel such frustration as it may be you have no grasp of the situation and that is why they continually feel frustrated in your company. It would be an excellent idea to spend some of your time looking at what is really going on. If, for instance, you stand there and laugh at the other person then that would indicate you are choosing to ignore what is going on, or it may be you believe you are there simply to listen and are unable to take on board what it is they are saying and how it reflects on you. Do you see the relevance of considering your impact on a situation that continues to repeat in your life? You may indeed be correct that the learning needed is on the part of the other person, but it is essential you spend a great deal of time considering whether you are in fact oblivious to the learning that is required on your part, especially if this keeps happening.

I would now like to take this step a little further. Having considered this and decided it's important to be a little more receptive to others, it then becomes necessary to examine your part in these situations. It may well be that by being less than understanding of what is going on you are adding fuel to the fire of another person's frustration, and so attempts need to be made on your part to listen a little more closely or ask a few more questions about how your behaviour is impacting on them. With luck the other person will give you some clues about what it is you are choosing to ignore. This would be particularly helpful as it would offer you some information about the areas of your life that need examination, and that will give you an opportunity to learn and grow.

It may be, having achieved this level of understanding, it becomes necessary to spend some time with yourself trying to understand the reasons you have been choosing to ignore this part of yourself. Having been in denial for some time there is clearly something hidden underneath that you are working extremely hard to avoid, and it is vital that whatever that is, is given a great deal of your time so you can try and understand and then do your best to learn and grow from this opportunity. It may be it takes a number of opportunities like this before you are able to achieve your learning, but all the while denial is in place it is impossible to learn and grow, and so once denial is removed a great many more opportunities will be open to you.

Appreciating the differences between people

I have said a number of times before how all of you are unique and on earth to learn lessons that are individual to each of you, and it is important to always remember that, as even on the occasions when two people are there to learn the same lesson they will be offered that lesson in different ways, and so it is often difficult to have a clear understanding of what it is you are there to learn. There are times when I think it is important to simply go along for the ride and to learn and grow from whatever is presented to you, instead of working hard to try and understand what you are there to learn. Every time an opportunity is presented to you is an opportunity to grow, and I cannot emphasise enough the importance of taking those opportunities and doing your best to learn from them. There are so many who, even with an understanding that they are there to learn and grow, choose to ignore opportunities because they have no wish to step outside their comfort zone. That helps no one as, having completed your life and been unable to achieve all you intended to achieve, you will have a great deal of frustration and disappointment with yourself as it was frustration that took you to earth in the first place. It will then become necessary to return in order to learn additional lessons and have further opportunities to grow. So you see it is in your very best interests to grab every opportunity offered to you, and to do your best to try to learn and grow from each of them.

All of us in spirit have a full understanding of the discomfort involved in this growth; however, it is the way it is and there is nothing we can do about that except encourage you to be brave and embrace the opportunities offered to you.

Standing up for yourself as a step towards reaching your potential

I think each of you needs to give yourself some time to consider the occasions in your life when you wished you were able to stand up for yourself rather more than you did. I am aware there may be some who are unable to recall these situations; however, I encourage you to do your best – it is only necessary to remember one or two. Then consider how you could have altered this situation given the information I have now given you. This is not an opportunity to be hard on yourself; it's simply one to become more aware of how to stand up for yourself. I think many of you have a number of skills, and I believe you all have the skill within you, to stand up for yourself. It is simply something you need to get used to, as this is a part of you that has become rather squashed over the years and needs a little guidance and an opportunity to allow it to flourish. It does of course require a level of bravery on your part, as when part of a person has been squashed for a period of time, to allow that part of themselves to return is difficult, as it is usually fear that has caused it to diminish and keeps it at bay, and so it is necessary to do your best to overcome that fear. It is important this is what you choose to do as each of you has the potential to be a well-rounded individual and not the type of person you currently are, which is a rather limited version of your true self. So, I would like you all to be as brave as you possibly can and allow that part of yourself to flourish and resume the position it once had before it was squashed. It is important you give yourself the opportunity to allow that part of yourself to redevelop, as your life will become considerably easier, and it will then be possible to focus your energies on areas of your life that need your attention. When I say that it may simply be that more attention needs to be offered in regard to enjoying yourself. All the efforts in this world are not necessarily hard work; they can be for something that is really rather pleasant. It is simply an opportunity for you to step forward and embrace the person you truly are, which is, after all, the reason you are all there.

I also think each of you needs to be more aware of how important it is to reach your full potential, because as we have mentioned before, the reason you are there is to learn and grow, and part of that growth means reaching your full potential. Each of you when you chose to incarnate on earth made a decision to develop yourself as much as possible in the hope of reaching your full potential, and when we talk of people reaching their full potential what we refer to is a person who is able to use all parts of their personality equally and easily.

This means they are able to deal with any situations offered to them. That does not mean these situations will necessarily be easy; what it does mean is you will have sufficient skills available to deal with any situation that is presented.

It also means you are able to take on board any additional skills you hoped to learn while you are there, and in that regard I am referring more to interests you wish to develop. So, do you see that, in order to reach your full potential, it is important to understand all your limitations and to try and remove them from your life? I hope that is clear, and that you all have an understanding of what it means to reach your full potential. It is something that for some will be remarkably easy; however, I am aware for many others it will require a great deal of courage and practice to be able to develop, grow and become the person they wished to be.

How to embrace your true self

This may sound a little repetitive; however, I think it's important to offer some information in the hope you are able to differentiate between standing up for yourself and embracing your true self, as there is indeed a difference. We have previously looked at how to stand up for yourself and learn the skills required in order to be rather more comfortable with yourself, but I think it's also important I offer some information on how to become more familiar with the person you hope to become.

Each of you when you incarnated on earth had a list of objectives you hoped to attain. Many of you had very long lists, which I confess is something I prefer people not to do as that tends to set some of you up for disappointment as it's not always easy to achieve so many goals. Standing up for yourself is the main criterion required in order to learn what you intend to learn. To be able to stand up for yourself and take on many of the events life throws at you gives you sufficient skills to deal with all that is presented to you. That does not necessarily mean everything will be easy; it simply means you will have the skills available. I hope that's clear as it is not possible to itemise the lessons that are undertaken and to offer solutions to each one as that would require a great many books; however, I believe if you are able to adopt a few techniques and skills it becomes considerably easier to learn and grow.

The person each of you hopes to be is within your grasp; however, a level of bravery is required as in order to embrace your true self it is necessary to step out of your comfort zone. That is all that's required, however, and while I appreciate it is a particularly uncomfortable experience it is nonetheless a stepping stone to embracing your true self. It is not as if you need to place yourself in mortal danger to achieve any of these lessons; it is simply feeling uncomfortable for a period of time. It may of course be that you choose a path and feel particularly uncomfortable, but unfortunately that path was not the correct one and so the process requires a repeat performance; however, you will become more comfortable with feeling uncomfortable and so it will be easier to become more accustomed to developing new avenues of experience. The reason you have made a decision to try and reach your full potential is because it will then be possible to associate with everybody in spirit you wish to associate with; it also allows you to stop returning to earth if that is your wish. Some of you choose to continue to return simply because you enjoy being there, and if that is your choice it is unlikely you will have so much to learn and so your life will be considerably easier. However, the majority choose never to return to earth again as we feel life on earth is hard given that you have so many chores to achieve simply to sustain yourselves, and in spirit we have none of that. To reach your full potential also allows you to become more involved in projects here in spirit that were previously denied to you, and that allows for a whole wealth of experience as the projects each of you is suited to vary and for the most part are extremely interesting; however your suitability for these projects depends on the development achieved on earth. So you see it's important to try and achieve what you intended to achieve, and to reach your potential. It may be many more lives are required for this potential to be reached; however, it is important to do your best to achieve as much as you possibly can while you are in this life in order to minimise the list of accomplishments that will be required next time – if, of course, you choose to return. It is not compulsory for everybody to learn on earth; it is simply something that is achieved considerably faster than if you were to remain in spirit.

How important it is to place a greater focus on developing your skills

When I talk of your skills I am referring particularly to what you went to earth to learn. That can be the learning required for your soul, or it can refer to the learning you have a desire to achieve while you are there; for instance, artistic skills or map-reading or perhaps how an engine works. There are a whole host of additional skills each of you has a desire to learn. It may be in your current life these are skills you are unaware of; however, it is likely throughout your life these skills will gradually become more important to learn and I would like to encourage each of you to do exactly that. As you become aware of skills you discover an interest in, I would like you to do your best to utilise that desire in the hope of learning any additional skills you intended to learn. There is no need to go out searching to determine what these skills are, as when the time is right your guides will encourage you to achieve them. It is important to listen to the voice which tries to encourage you to learn something new and then to embrace it and do your best to learn what is desired. It is very likely when you are able to fully embrace this skill your life will become somewhat easier, you will have a sense of balance and there will likely be a feeling of pleasure and achievement as it will gradually allow you to become the person you hoped to be.

    I also think it is important to spend some time considering all the things in life that have an interest for you and then select a few and perhaps pursue them. It may be your life is currently so full, perhaps with bringing up your family or dealing with situations, that it is not possible to consider taking on other interests. However, it is never the wrong moment to give these interests some thought as the day will come when you will have more time on your hands and it is important to be ready to embrace that opportunity instead of lamenting times past.

The current trend for self-acceptance

I am aware there is something of a trend in your society at the moment to try and gain a greater acceptance of not only the person you are, but those around you. However, I have a degree of reservation with this as I have no wish for you to accept yourself the way you are as it is likely many of you will resist the need to learn and grow and will simply appreciate the difficulties you have in certain situations rather than employing techniques to change them. It is far more important to embrace the changes required in order to reach your full potential than it is to accept the way you are and resist the necessity to change. I am aware this line of thinking may go against a great deal of what you have been taught; however, it is important to be kind to yourself and appreciate the changes needed within you, and then to employ methods that allow you to do that. It is necessary to be extremely kind to yourself as you go through this learning as there are many who choose to be particularly hard on themselves when they realise they were unable to achieve all they had hoped; please remember it is all learning and it may be necessary to be unable to learn successfully the first few times. There may, however, be a great deal of learning that occurs within that process, and so when you do eventually learn the lesson it will have a greater depth than if you had been able to learn it at the first opportunity. Being unable to succeed the first time enables your learning to be richer and deeper, and so I would like you to consider that the next time you choose to give yourself a hard time due to your lack of learning.

 A great deal of energy is wasted by many of you on earth in giving yourself a hard time when there is no need and nothing to be gained; in fact there is a great deal to be lost as so many maintain a lower level of self-esteem. So, tell me what is to be gained? Nothing as far as I can tell.

More on the current trend for acceptance

Why acceptance in itself is a particularly hot topic at the moment I am unclear. There is of course a great deal to be gained by accepting those around you, as their learning needs to occur at their own pace. While acceptance of other people allows you to have a better relationship with them, I do have a level of reservation, as accepting others the way they are allows them to remain stuck in whatever situation they find themselves in. It's essential you are able to offer encouragement in the hope of furthering their need to learn and grow. When I say that, I do not mean for you to begin telling another person how to live their life; I simply mean that when a person offers a suggestion for how they think they may be able to improve their life, or uses you as a sounding board with the aim of seeing how you feel in regard to their development, I would like you to offer encouragement and possibly some information, if that is available to you, in the hope they will embrace the learning that is available to them. This does not mean you need to work hard to find ways to allow them to grow, it simply means offering encouragement. I am not sure that simply accepting a person for the way they are is an entirely appropriate thing to do, especially as this limits their development. It also limits your own development if an acceptance of the person you are, warts and all, is allowed to continue throughout your life. I hope that is clear, and you understand the point I am trying to make in regard to acceptance. Any kind of development is something of a struggle, and it is easy to simply say, 'I accept myself the way I am' and not choose to allow yourself to develop. It may be you do this through fear, as it is easier to accept your inabilities than it is to try and embrace a level of development; however, that is not acceptable.

16 How to Make the Most of the Opportunities Presented to You

I am aware I have covered this topic previously; however, there is more I would like to add. It is important each of you is aware that a great many opportunities are offered throughout your life on earth, and I would like to draw your attention to a number of them I have already mentioned as that will save me repeating what I have previously said. I have deliberately chosen to deliver this information at this point as I thought it important for you to gain a little more knowledge before I cover what it is I wish to say. I think you need to have a greater understanding of all that is offered to you throughout your life on earth. I also think it is important more of you are aware of just how much work goes into ensuring you have as many opportunities as possible to achieve your aims, as your guides spend a great deal of time working to ensure it is possible for a significant number of opportunities to be presented to you. This is done by presenting the opportunities that would benefit you the most in a way that you are able to recognise as being beneficial to you. There are occasions when people have decided a particular avenue of learning is important to them as they may have spent many lifetimes trying to learn a specific lesson which has proved fruitless, and they reach a level of determination where they wish for a number of complications in their life to try and ensure they are able to achieve the learning they wish to achieve. For instance, if a person is struggling to learn to care for themselves in a kind and loving way, it may be a particular illness needs to occur in order for them to take greater care of their life and health, or it may be a high level of independence has been woven into the fabric of a person's life which is simply no good for a life either on earth or here in spirit. So it is important that person has a greater appreciation of the need to have others in their life, and so a particular injury may befall them where they need others to care for them or at least offer their assistance. We hope in these instances people are able to have a greater opportunity to learn what it was they intended to learn.

Always when such drastic measures are presented, the person has been offered a great many opportunities beforehand to learn that particular lesson; however, for some this proves to be insufficient and it is necessary for us to ensure either an illness or an injury befalls a person in the hope that the lesson will be learned. It is also necessary to understand this will have been arranged with the individual before their incarnation on earth, and so while we appreciate these events come as something of a surprise in your human life, they are in fact planned, and the spiritual part of yourself is fully aware of the consequences of your actions. So you see it is of the utmost importance each of you makes a great deal of effort to learn and grow while you are on earth in the hope of avoiding many of these illnesses and injuries that may befall you.

We are aware these are harsh lessons to learn; however, I would like to reiterate that they have been planned by you in the hope of achieving a greater amount of growth and learning. Many of you become desperate to achieve that growth despite being given a great many opportunities.

I have previously mentioned that if people live particularly unkind lives and are rather objectionable to others there will be repercussions, and it is possible these repercussions may take the form of lifelong illnesses. It is hoped that enduring these types of obstacles will offer you a greater level of compassion and kindness for other people, as these are often things that were missing in a person's life. We believe if a person has a life to live that is particularly gruelling it gives them an opportunity to observe what many others endure on earth, and we have, in the past, found this to be a particularly effective way to encourage people to be more compassionate. It is important that as many people as possible who are in spirit have a great deal of kindness, benevolence and understanding for the struggles of others, and not only those in spirit but those who are walking the earth too. I am aware it may upset some of you that such harsh consequences are meted out to people, but again I remind you that each person who endures such an ordeal has agreed to it; in fact there are occasions when they have asked for it in the hope of achieving greater levels of growth.

Like every society, it is necessary for us to have a number of rules that everybody chooses to live by, and kindness, compassion, benevolence and love are the ones we choose to live our life by. It is our hope that, over time, more of this will be evident on earth. Great efforts are being made by us in spirit to try and ensure this is the case; however, it is taking many years to achieve. Despite that, we continue in our endeavours to try and ensure more of you have opportunities to allow these qualities to develop.

There are those amongst you who, when illness or injury befalls you, choose to become extremely angry, and while we understand the reasons, it serves no useful purpose. It is important to spend a considerable amount of time trying to understand the reasons why these particular experiences have happened to you, and then do your best to correct them. It may be your lifestyle was particularly erratic when it came to caring for yourself and so it became necessary for your priorities to be altered so that you are able to receive a greater level of care and love from yourself, or it may be that it's important for you to adopt kinder ways in caring for other people, or it may be necessary for you to appreciate that all people are on earth to learn and grow. To be given the opportunity to achieve exactly that, it is important you are able to take up the reins and understand the reasons for what ails you and then work harder to try and ensure you are able to overcome it. Once that particular understanding has occurred and you choose to correct the way you have been living, it may be whatever it is that has befallen you will ease and it may even resolve; however, that is not always the case and it may be necessary to endure the consequences for the rest of your life. Do you see how important it is to be kind to yourself and to those around you, and to appreciate that your time on earth is truly a gift that needs to be savoured and appreciated?

The importance of caring for yourself

When people are young and their bodies are developing they have a great deal of flexibility and so it is easy for many of you to abuse yourselves in various ways. This may take the form of excessive exercise or no exercise, or it may be excessive alcohol consumption or drug use, or excessive eating or heavily restricted eating; there are many ways to take your youth and young, flexible body for granted. However, it is simply not possible for this to continue. It is extremely important you are able to adopt a policy of being kind to yourself and your body in order to ensure it is able to last your lifetime. So, it may be, for those of you who choose to drink alcohol excessively, that opportunities will be offered to you to perhaps ease up or eventually stop your drinking. It depends on how excessively you choose to drink or how many lives you have been subjecting yourself to this particular form of abuse, and it may be we ensure a number of incidents occur which we hope will concern you enough to stop you drinking so much. Over time the severity of these incidents will grow in the hope you will eventually realise how important it is to take greater care of yourself. If these incidents are ignored and a decision is made on your part to continue drinking then it may be necessary for us to offer either an intolerance to alcohol or perhaps an alcohol-related illness in the hope that will encourage you to stop the abuse. If this does not work then we will continue to increase the events that befall you in the hope you will eventually realise it is important to stop drinking.

We appreciate almost everybody who drinks does so for a reason and in the hope of avoiding looking at certain parts of their life. It is necessary that the crutches you choose to use are removed in the hope you will spend a much greater time looking at events in your life that have brought you to where you currently are, and that by doing so you are able to gain a greater understanding and learning from them. There are any number of ways each of you can choose to work to ignore or suppress these events; they do not need to be alcohol related. However, I am aware those of you reading this will be aware on some level if this is something that applies to you, and you will know if there are events in your life you are trying to ignore. It is important to find a way to allow those events to step forward and receive attention as within them is a significant amount of learning that can be achieved, and while you were in spirit it was your hope these events would cause you to learn a great deal.

It may be extremely difficult living with this knowledge, which is of course why you chose to suppress it. If you find that to be the case then it is necessary to find some kind of support in the form of perhaps a counsellor or psychotherapist who will be able to guide you with the aim of understanding the events that have occurred. You do not necessarily need to find a therapist; it may be you simply find a person who is able to listen, or another avenue to provide yourself with the necessary understanding. There are many ways you could do this and I invite each of you to be as creative and imaginative as possible in the hope of finding a way that works for you. It is important to work hard to gain a greater level of understanding for the reasons that brought you to this excessive behaviour in the hope of attaining the learning and growth you set out on this journey to achieve. It is also important, when you do find yourself in a position of achieving this learning and understanding, that you are able to fully appreciate what you have achieved, as to have reached a point where it was necessary for your learning to be so hard is an indication that this is something you have tried over many lifetimes to learn, and so it is highly beneficial if you are able to fully grasp how wondrous it is to have finally reached your goal.

We would also like to reassure you that, upon your realisation of what it is you are there to learn and be in a position to develop, there is an enormous amount of celebration that goes on here in spirit, not only among the guides who work hard to try and encourage you, but also family and friends who have passed back to spirit and are all here trying to encourage you to achieve this learning. It is rather unfortunate that it requires you to return to spirit to appreciate the celebration that has occurred; however, when your time finally comes to return home there will be further celebrations that you will be able to participate in, as it is important a great deal of acknowledgement is afforded to any achievement that has proved to be extremely difficult to learn. In fact anyone who learns any of their lessons has a great deal to celebrate, as we feel life on earth is hard and it is important you are all able to appreciate what you have achieved.

17 How to Make More Time for Yourself

There is a great deal I could say about how to make more time for yourself as we see so many of you with lives filled with chores, many of which are unnecessary, and it would be to the benefit of all to find time for yourself. This can take the form of fun and enjoyment, which I will go into greater detail about in the next chapter; however, I would also like you to find time for yourself, where it's possible, to be alone. I am aware many of you struggle with being alone, but this is for a predetermined period of time and it is something I would like each of you to do on a daily basis, if that's possible.

I feel there are certain habits that it's important to participate in daily, as not only does that ensure the habit receives the attention it is due, but in many ways it is easier to maintain if it is a daily practice. If a person chooses to do something every other day and life becomes busier, that thing is often one of the first to be dropped. It is essential you take time on a daily basis to recharge your batteries and ensure you are able to put the demands of your life into perspective. It need only be half an hour a day, and for those who have particularly busy lives then perhaps allow twenty minutes, but no less as you need to place a value on the time you are willing to give yourself. I would like it if you were able to find a place where you can be undisturbed; it may be necessary to be creative, but I would encourage you to do it. During this period of isolation, take a few slow, deep breaths, holding between the inspiration and expiration for a count of four. Then when you have done that, ensure you are sitting comfortably and upright with your eyes closed and do your best to focus on your breathing. It may be you need to employ other tricks to keep your mind calm, and for some it may be necessary to imagine yourself surrounded by foliage or sea, or any place in the world that offers you a great deal of serenity; and as you do that, try to prevent yourself from being distracted by all the events going on in your life. I believe the best time of day for this to be accomplished is as soon as you wake, as many of you have not yet got fully into your stride of listing all the things that need to be accomplished in that day. As you do this it allows your mind to calm and cease worrying about all those jobs.

Focusing on your breathing offers an opportunity to choose to ignore all the chores that wish to overtake you and encompass your mind. Instead, continue to focus on your breathing and perhaps the feeling that conjures up in your body. Some of you may like to imagine how your breath is spreading throughout your entire body, providing it with the oxygen it needs to survive. The choice is yours and it may require a number of attempts before you are fully able to find the process that works best for you, and then spend that period doing exactly that. As you become aware of decisions that need to be made or lists that need to be accomplished, simply acknowledge them and then let them go. You may wish to say something like, 'Thank you; I will come back to that later', or imagine a tennis racket and hit that subject away as you would a ball. There are many techniques it is possible to adopt; it simply requires ingenuity on your part and a willingness to give this very precious gift to yourself.

For those with particularly busy lives this is something that will require a great deal of practice. The benefits are truly enormous as you will find your life calms considerably. It is surprising how much of your time is wasted worrying about all the things you believe are important, and to relax a little provides you with a great deal more time throughout your day in ways that it's difficult to imagine if you choose not to participate in this form of contemplation. Simply offering yourself this time each day is a truly magnificent way to alter your life.

If there was only one thing I was able, throughout this book, to convince you to try it would be this: spending a part of every day in quiet contemplation. I think before a decision is made on your part to dismiss this it is important you are able to try it out for a significant period of time in order to determine the benefits it has in your life. Only after a number of weeks of practice, if you find there are insufficient benefits, should you consider dismissing it;

however, I do not believe that will happen. If you are able to offer this to yourself for, say, three weeks then I believe the benefits will be so enormous there will be nothing to be gained by removing this practice from your life. I hope each of you will be willing to take this on board and give yourself that time each day in the hope of improving your quality of life.

18 How to Have More Fun in Your Life

I would like to speak to you about how to have as much fun in your life as it's possible for you to have. I am aware there are many of you who are particularly skilled at this; however, there are also many who struggle a great deal with it. It is important many more of you spend a great deal of your time enjoying yourself as it makes your life so much easier. I am aware I have touched on this subject previously, but I would like to give you more information.

Some of you have an awareness of the many people on earth who are struggling a great deal with the circumstances they find themselves in, to the point where it often elicits a level of guilt on your part that you are in a position to have a lot of fun and they simply are not. However, I would like to draw your attention to the fact that each of you is there for your own learning and it is vital it is not hampered by the learning of anybody else. It is also necessary to realise that if others choose not to enjoy themselves, or are not in a position to enjoy themselves, then that is entirely down to them. It is very much your responsibility to ensure you have a great deal of fun and enjoyment in your life. It is simply not possible to avoid it out of guilt and others to find any benefit in that. So you see it's important you place your focus on your own life and leave others to theirs. Even those of you who live in countries where there is a great deal of hardship and suffering need to find ways to enjoy yourselves, and I appreciate for some of you that will be extremely difficult. However, I cannot urge you enough to try and find the lighter aspects of life and enjoy those moments it's possible to enjoy. It is of the utmost importance each of you has a degree of fun and enjoyment in your life as this offers access to so much more, and frequently provides a platform through which to make a great deal more of your life. I am hopeful with this consideration in mind many of you will be able to focus greater levels of attention on doing exactly that and making more of your life in regard to fun and enjoyment. It is important this topic is given greater priority in order to make more of your life on earth.

What fun and enjoyment can offer you

This I have covered briefly already; however, I would like to add a little more to this subject. Not only does having more fun in your life allow your energy to lighten and become more appealing to others, which enables you to attract the company of other people, but it also makes your own life feel lighter and easier. It allows your life to move along in a way that is infinitely more pleasant. It means there are a great many things you will be able to accomplish that are unavailable to someone who chooses not to have fun and enjoyment in their life. This is because their energy becomes heavier; it is far less pleasant to have a person with heavy energy in your circle of friends or as a colleague at work, as it requires a considerable effort to try and find ways to lift your own energy when you are in their company. The most obvious way, as I have been trying to explain, is to have a great deal more fun in your life, and this can be done in so many ways. One of those ways is to find things you enjoy doing and do them regardless of the excuses you are able to find to avoid doing them. Put yourself out, especially to begin with, to find ways to enjoy yourself. There are other ways, and one of those is to take classes on subjects you enjoy. This ensures that at particular times each week you are able to do something you thoroughly enjoy doing, and with luck over time you will make friends with people who also enjoy themselves in that way.

Another suggestion to consider is to perhaps offer some of your time for the benefit of others. This may seem a rather strange way to enjoy yourself; however, it is surprising how much fun can be achieved when you are working with people who are less advantaged than you as it brings not only a greater appreciation for your own life but also much more pleasure to the lives of others simply by offering a little of your time. There are many who believe this to be a particularly hard way to enjoy yourself; however, I would like to suggest an effort be made on your part before being certain that is in fact the case. It is important more of you feel inclined to offer some of your time each week for the benefit of other people in the hope of not only finding a level of fun and enjoyment in your own life, but offering kindness to others. You will be surprised at the effects this has as it is possible for the lives of all of you to be uplifted, and I am hopeful that is something many will try to implement as there are a great many people who struggle with this life, and simply by offering a little of your time you are able to lighten the load, not only in your own life but in the lives of others.

Another way I think would be highly beneficial is to perhaps find ways where it is possible to be with others who are also enjoying themselves. In this instance I am thinking along the lines of people who choose to dance, or maybe do some form of keep-fit or sport. When people are moving around a lot that too helps to lift your energy and there can be benefits to that. All of you will feel your energy lifting considerably as you move, and that in itself offers fun.

Another way to enjoy yourself is to try and focus your energies on a particular subject that interests you and then find a number of other people who feel the same. There is a great deal to be gained by finding others who enjoy the same things as you as it offers an opportunity to speak with like-minded people, and this will help curry a great deal more interest in that subject. It will offer insights and information that it's not always possible to develop yourself.

So, I have offered a number of suggestions to introduce a greater amount of fun and enjoyment into your life;

however, the single most important thing I need each of you to do is to take up the mantle of finding things you enjoy doing and going ahead and implementing them. It is easy with your busy lives these days to find excuses not to participate in these; however, they are without doubt excuses and it's important to work to make a place in your life where it's possible to enjoy yourself.

So, I would very much like to encourage all of you to focus a great deal of your attention on this subject and then implement the decisions you have made, and as a result you will find your life becomes considerably easier.

19 Further Information About How to Make the Most of Opportunities Offered to You

This may sound familiar; however, it is something I would like to build upon and I am hoping you will bear with me. It is essential to be aware of the importance of making the most of the opportunities presented to you, and I have gone into some detail about how that is possible. However, there are a great many opportunities open to you that only you can take advantage of, and I would like to encourage you to do exactly that. As I have said previously, there are many lessons you can learn throughout your lifetimes on earth and it is important to appreciate these types of things. It is simply not appropriate for me to give you a long list of all the things it's possible to learn; however, there is a remarkably simple way to have a clear understanding of what is on the list of things *you* need to learn; and that is, all the things that offer you a level of fear. All those situations you choose to avoid as you believe they will lead to discomfort, or a challenge you are unwilling to undertake, are, for the most part, exactly the things you are there to learn, and while each of you made a decision before you incarnated about the number of lessons you hoped to learn in this life, it is likely there are a great many more yet for you to learn. So, I would like to encourage you to spend some time considering that there is much you can do to promote your own learning without the help of your guides. Your guides are only there to offer you guidance in regard to what you requested of them before your incarnation; however, for most of you there is considerably more yet to learn and that is something you have the potential to develop yourself, as I believe there is always a great deal of potential for learning that is not necessarily in your remit for this life.

You are now aware there are many lessons each person needs to learn, and while it is not always possible to learn all those lessons in one lifetime, it is possible to learn more than you had originally planned to learn. I would like to encourage you to work hard to embrace situations in which you have a level of reticence or fear and then spend some time considering whether these types of situations have appeared in your life previously. If that is the case I would like you to be extremely brave and embrace that situation, and to do your best to overcome those fears.

It may of course be that in your attempt you are able to respond in a way you have not yet done but which may be the incorrect solution; however, that will give you a greater level of courage to attempt that scenario again. It also provides additional information as to how not to respond on another occasion. Do you see how important it is to embrace all the things in your life which offer a degree of difficulty to you?

There is a great deal to be gained by working to overcome challenges that keep occurring in your life. There is simply no need to ever stop learning, and it may be you find yourself in older age and continue to be aware of situations that offer challenges, and I would like to assure you that you really are never too old to take advantage of opportunities that are offered. If you feel able to attempt such challenges it is something you will appreciate a great deal on your return home as it may well be possible to bank a few lessons; this means you have learned more than you anticipated and there will be no need to relearn those lessons in a future life. Do you see how much there is to be gained by taking up the mantle and being as brave as you can possibly be in situations that offer you something of a challenge? It is essential, however, that these challenges do not put you in any danger as that is not the point of learning and growing. It is important to be aware of the need to protect and care for your own life at all times, and any fears that are presented to you where your life may potentially be in danger are not the kind of fears I am speaking about. I hope that is clear as I have no wish for any of you to put yourself in any situation where you or your life may be at risk.

The importance of continuing to develop throughout your life

Many of you, throughout your life, go through periods of learning about yourself. These situations tend to occur when there has been a significant change in your life. It may be a relationship of some kind has ended abruptly and you are trying to achieve a greater level of understanding of the reasons for that, and I would like to encourage you to make the most of that learning and to do your best to allow that learning to continue beyond your current level of understanding. It is important more of you work hard in your attempts to understand yourself and try to gain a greater level of understanding about why certain situations keep presenting themselves to you. I hope I have made it clear earlier in this book why that is; however, I would like you to continue in your endeavours to keep an open mind and further develop your understanding in a great many different ways, and not only those that allow you to understand a particular situation a little better.

It is necessary to keep working to learn and understand in the hope of becoming a far more rounded individual. I am also hopeful it will be possible to be aware that you have a great deal more yet to learn, as there are many of you who feel that so long as your lives are going along reasonably smoothly there is no need to present additional challenges to yourself. There are many who are keen to have lives with little excitement or challenge, as there seems to be a belief that if life is somewhat uneventful then you must be doing a great deal right, and that is simply not the case. Nobody is there to have an easy life, and it is important, if you find yourself in that situation, that you are able to recognise there may need to be a little more effort on your part in order to achieve a greater level of learning and growth. Do you see how important it is to take greater control over your own life, and to appreciate you are there to learn and grow and make the most of all the situations presented to you, as so many choose to avoid anything that offers any kind of challenge?

How important it is to take up the mantle and be as brave as you can be

It is easy to read this book and appreciate your life could do with a few extra challenges. The hard part is putting that into action, and I have a few suggestions about how to achieve that.

I am aware that for many of you a challenge causes something of a concern; however, how much is there to lose when you put yourself in the position of learning? It may be you experience some discomfort, or those around you are surprised you have chosen to take a particular path or respond in a way that makes you feel particularly uncomfortable; however, I would like to impress upon you how much you truly have to gain by responding in different ways and achieving a level of learning. I think all of you are likely to feel discomfort in situations that offer opportunities to learn; however, I cannot stress enough how important it is to embrace those opportunities and offer this gift to yourself. While you may feel all kinds of emotions when you accept these challenges, the benefit to yourself is truly enormous. Not only do you find your life becomes easier, but also on your return home there is an overwhelming sense of success, and that will feed you for many months, and on occasions, years. There is no greater joy available to anybody than what they experience when they realise what they have achieved. Life on earth is never easy and we in spirit are fully aware that simply living on earth provides its own challenges. So for you to not only achieve a life there, but also achieve a number of the lessons you hoped to learn, on your return fills all of us, as well as yourself, with enormous pleasure and satisfaction. I hope you are able to see, or at least have a better idea of, what you can achieve if you are only able to find some extra bravery, which you all have, and take up that mantle and achieve higher-than-anticipated levels of learning. If you are able to achieve this task it will be possible to further your progression once you return home to spirit.

I think it is important you are able not only to embrace your bravery, but try and encourage it in yourself, and I have a technique which I hope will help you to develop this skill. Bravery does not necessarily require you to be a hero; nor does it mean a great deal of achievement is needed – there is in fact a great deal of bravery required in many of the smaller things which occur within your life. Some of you may feel somewhat reticent to offer your help to another person simply because you believe they may snap back at you, or you are intruding on their space, or you feel a particular situation has nothing to do with you. However, I would like to encourage you to try and be a little braver by offering your help. It may well be the other person does not require your help, but the point of the exercise is to be brave enough to offer it, and I am hopeful that over time, if you are able to practise in smaller opportunities like this, your levels of bravery will gradually grow, and when you are faced with a situation that includes a great deal of learning the step that is required for you to take is not as massive as it was previously. Instead, as your bravery has been exercised a number of times, there will be a much greater level of development, and so taking another step that requires a degree of bravery is not quite the huge step it was to begin with. So, each time you are considering volunteering yourself for something, perhaps take that a little step further and embrace the opportunity.

If you find yourself knocked back then so be it; the important part of the exercise was to offer your help or your time or whatever it was you chose to offer, and even though you may feel a little let down, the exercise was nonetheless a huge success. Remember that, as I suspect there are some of you who will choose instead to focus on the fact that what you offered was not taken up, but that was not the point of the exercise. The point was to overcome your reticence in order to exercise your bravery for the gain of others. I hope I have made that clear as I have no wish for any of you to focus on the negative part and lose any confidence that has previously been gained.

I think it is important to accept that not every opportunity you choose to embrace will result in success. I am aware a lack of success often results in less inclination to attempt something similar again, and it can, on occasions, reduce your confidence in life generally. That is indeed a shame as many of you have shown a great deal of bravery in attempting a particular exercise to begin with, and it is important to focus your mind on what you have achieved. It may be you have given your all to a particular situation in the hope of success and yet success was not what was delivered to you; however, even within that a great deal of learning can occur and it is necessary considerable focus is given to that. It is important each of you is able to celebrate what you have achieved by putting yourself forward. It matters not whether success is achieved at the end, as the actual success was in the journey and not the final outcome, and I hope you will remember that as we see so many struggling when they have not achieved what they hoped to achieve. Yet we are able to observe the enormity of your success, and somehow that is the part of the situation many of you are unable to see. Often we are celebrating the huge amount of learning that has been achieved and yet you are commiserating with yourself, full of misery and upset due to what you believe to be a failure, and for the most part that is simply not the case. Life is one long learning experience and learning is the reason you are on earth. None of you are there to achieve one success after another, although I appreciate there are those who appear to achieve exactly that; however, I can assure you there are parts of anybody's life that bring them considerable struggle. It may be they choose to mask this part of themself or these events that have occurred in their life, but I can guarantee they have formed a part of their life.

The importance of achieving your lessons

I have spoken a number of times previously on the importance of learning your lessons and I have given a number of indications as to how it's possible to do that;

however, I would like to offer one more suggestion and that is for you all to have a better idea of the value of failure.

Many of you choose to focus your lives on your successes and few of you ever consider the value of failure. If you worked hard to make something reach fruition and it does not, then that is because it was never meant to be and it is important to remember that, as I believe there are many amongst you who determine the value of your life according to the number of successes you have managed to achieve. That is something all of you would do well to try and correct as your successes are a poor indication of the value of your life and what you have achieved. There is a great deal of learning in a lack of success, and very often more learning can be achieved than if a person is successful, so I think it is important to focus more of your attention on what you did achieve where the initial appearance is one of failure. When you become aware of a lack of success there is often a period of adjustment that needs to take place and we understand that; however, once that has taken place, or even towards the end of it, it would be an excellent idea to sit down quietly and consider all you have gained from this lack of success and celebrate that. It may be you need to be particularly open-minded and appreciative of all the effort you put into this event. It is important time is spent giving yourself a pat on the back and a great deal of encouragement for all the things you did in fact achieve. I believe it to be of the utmost importance this opportunity is afforded to you as it is so often the case that you focus your energies on your lack of apparent success, and that is a waste of time. If there are scenarios where you have put a great deal of energy into a particular thing and it was either not achieved or another person's idea was considered superior to your own, then it was simply never the plan for you to achieve that success. For you the learning was in the journey, and I hope you are all able to consider that and to offer yourself a great deal of time to savour what you have achieved on your journey.

I would like for each of you to focus more of your attention on the journey towards either your success or your perceived lack of success, as I think it is important to have a greater understanding of the learning that is achieved. We work particularly hard in spirit to try and ensure you are offered as many learning opportunities as possible, and it may well be that we have arranged for your learning to be encompassed in your attempts to succeed at a particular aim; however, it was never our intention for you to achieve that aim. It was simply important for us to ensure you were given a number of opportunities to learn, and it is hoped that when such an event is presented to you, you are able to appreciate how many opportunities were involved in that journey. I am aware I am repeating myself a little here; however, I think it is essential each of you becomes aware that the important part of the exercise is the journey, as so many get hung up on the success or lack of it, and that is immaterial. I'm not sure I have so much desire to pursue this any further as I hope I have made that point as clear as I possibly can.

How to focus your attention on achieving your aims

I believe many of you intend to complete your aims but find yourselves too busy to actually do so, and I am hopeful I can offer a suggestion as to how it may be possible to put your intentions into practice. The suggestion I have is simply to diarise that intention. For those of you whose lives are rather busy, when you are available to pursue an aim there is a tendency to take advantage of the free time by doing remarkably little; but I believe if you are able to diarise these intentions it will make it considerably easier to put them into practice. Once your intention is diarised it will, I believe, offer a greater incentive to action that intention, and I am hopeful that is what many of you will do.

20 How to Allow Yourself to Have a Good Life

The importance of accepting responsibility for your own behaviour

I am aware many of you choose to partake in various events within your lives, and I think it's important to consider whose decision it is to partake in those events. It may be you are invited along with a group of people, or it may be you choose to attend a particular event alone; however, the decision of whether or not to attend is yours and yours alone, unless of course you are a child, in which case it becomes the responsibility of your parents, though I am not sure there will be so many children reading this book.

For the most part each of you is responsible for your decision to attend a particular event, and so if there are any mishaps that occur at that event it is very much your responsibility for being there. It may be while you are there another person chooses to inflict their behaviour upon you, and in those instances the responsibility for the results of that behaviour are very much with that person – provided of course you had no part in eliciting that reaction from them.

There are many of you who choose to place the blame for any incident on another person and it is remarkably easy to do; however, ultimately the responsibility is your own for simply being in that particular place.

This is something I would like to elaborate on as so many people in society today seem unable to accept responsibility for their actions, and it is important this stops as you are all responsible for yourselves at all times, unless of course you are a child. If you find another person is inflicting less-than-favourable behaviour on you then it is your responsibility to remove yourself from that situation. (There are exceptions to this, for instance, rapidly developing situations where it's physically not possible to remove yourself.) Or if you find other people are working to inflict their decisions on you and you wholeheartedly disagree with what they are saying, then again it is your responsibility to remove yourself. This may seem remarkably simple and I feel sure many of you find yourselves in rather complicated situations where it is not so easy to extricate yourself; however, I would like you to bear what I have said in mind and, where possible, do your best to disentangle yourself from any situation where you are unable to accept responsibility for your own behaviour.

If the situation you find yourself in entails behaving in a way that does not sit well with you then it is important to remove yourself, but if you find the behaviours of others are in fact much how you would react yourself then it is not so necessary to remove yourself, but it is necessary to accept responsibility for having chosen to remain where you are. It is never acceptable to action the requests of others and then blame them when things go wrong, as it was you who actioned those requests. If you wholeheartedly disagreed with them then it was important for you to either refuse to action them or remove yourself from that situation. Do you see? Are you able to comprehend the importance of being responsible for your own behaviour? I am hopeful you have a clear idea of how important it is to be in charge of your own behaviour and actions, as it is unacceptable to behave in a particular way and then blame your actions on another when things do not go as well as you thought they would. This is a particularly important point I wish to make as there are many of you who choose to blame your own behaviours on the decisions of others, and that is something that needs to stop as each one of you, once you have reached adulthood, is responsible for yourself.

You will find if you are able to accept responsibility for your own behaviour that your life feels more your own. Each of you will stop being a pawn in other people's exercises and become the king or queen of your own life. There will be occasions when it becomes necessary to carry out the wishes of another, and when that occasion arrives you need to consider whether or not this request is acceptable, and if it is then by all means action it. However, if that is not the case then it's important you do not follow through with that particular action, as each of you needs to be responsible for your own life and your own behaviours. In time this will stop you being dependent on the whims of others, your life will take on a strength of its own and ultimately prevent you from being the victim of the decisions of other people. This is a particularly important chapter and I hope I am making it clear to you how necessary it is to be responsible for your own behaviour, as I think there are many people who choose to action a particular behaviour and then when it does not work out quite as they hoped they blame another person. This occurs a great deal in politics, where there is a tendency for everybody to blame everybody else for decisions that do not turn out quite as people had anticipated, and I feel sure many of you are familiar with that; however, it is the responsibility of each person when they cast their vote to accept the outcome of their intentions, and I hope that is something each of you will do from now on as once you have reached adulthood there is nobody but yourself who is responsible for your life.

The importance of making changes to your life in order to accept responsibility for your own life and your own decisions

Each of you needs to be aware that you are in charge of your own life and it is your responsibility to steer your life in the direction you wish to go, however, there may be occasions when you are held to account, which is something that comes with the responsibility of your life. By that I mean when you make a particular decision and choose to put it into action it is not always found to be entirely acceptable by other people, and if that action did in fact have negative consequences you will be required to try and explain the reasons why you made that decision, and it is important you are able to be clear. If you made the decision on a whim and it had a significant impact on the lives of others then it is likely you will be called to account; however, if you made the decision based on a number of criteria and the results of that decision did not pan out quite as you hoped, you are then able to advise others of the reasons you chose that particular route. This is essential. It may be there are criteria that it's necessary to abide by, in which case if there is a succession of events which do not pan out as hoped due to these criteria then it may become necessary to instigate proceedings to amend them as it is unacceptable for people to have a consistently poor decision-making process that they must abide by. It may be there is a considerable amount of resistance to this; however, it is extremely important for you to accept responsibility for the decisions you are making and to ensure your decision-making process is based on valid criteria. If that is not the case then it is necessary to make changes as the buck has to stop with the person who made that decision, even though it may not necessarily be you who determined those criteria. Do you see how important it is to feel that your criteria for determining a course of action are indeed appropriate? I am hopeful I have made that clear as it is essential you are all able to accept responsibility for your own actions and not blame others when things go wrong.

There are those amongst you who find yourselves in situations where the decisions of others are forced upon you, and it is of the utmost importance that you are able to either alter that situation or walk away. I appreciate for some of you this will require a great deal of courage, but I would like to impress upon you the benefits you will reap once you have instigated this process. It is necessary for each of you to be the maker of the decisions that affect your life, or to at least accept the decisions that are made for you. It is never acceptable to action the decisions of others and then blame them when it goes wrong, and if you find yourself consistently in that position then you need to either remove yourself from that situation or be more responsible about taking on board what you are being encouraged to take on board, and by that, I mean stand up for yourself and speak your truth. I would like more of you to do exactly that and to be aware of the importance of it in your own life. To be able to stand by your own decisions and the decisions of others that you choose to accept and action has a profound effect on your life. It's important each of you is able to be responsible for your own life and the decisions you choose to make, and to have a list of criteria that are important to you, and live your life according to them. It is important you are the person who guides your life in the direction you wish to go and for no one else to do that for you.

An idea about how to take more responsibility for your actions

I am hopeful you will now be getting an indication of how important it is to be the instigator of your own behaviour and to do this with a responsibility that is worthy of the decisions you are making; however, I suspect there are a number of you who will struggle with this concept as spending a great many years at the beck and call of others means it is difficult to become responsible for your own actions. I have a suggestion for how I think it will be possible to gradually be in a position to live your life according to your own set of criteria.

For those who struggle with this I would like to encourage you to spend some of your time contemplating what's important for you in life. It may be important to be able to live comfortably with yourself and so it is necessary to make a decision and feel comfortable living with the effects of it; however, it may be you have a desire to be in a position of being responsible for a great many people in the hope of making your country a better place to live, in which case your decision-making will be considerably different to that of somebody who simply wants to live a life they are comfortable with. Or it may be you have a desire to run a company that seeks to improve the lives of others, in which case the decisions you make need to be made with that focus in mind. So, it is important that each of you, when you make a decision, is able to filter it through those particular criteria and decide whether or not it is an appropriate decision to make, and when you have made that decision, to then go ahead and action it. If, in the fullness of time, it proves to be a decision that was not necessarily beneficial, then it is important to accept responsibility and perhaps amend your decision or be in a position to justify it. What is not acceptable is to blame your decision on your circumstances or on other people, as it was in fact you who made that decision. This does of course mean that if it was a particularly good decision, then the beneficial aspects will fall on your shoulders also, and it is important to accept any praise or congratulations that come as a result. You may wish to appreciate others who chose to fulfil that particular decision with you; however, it is also essential to appreciate what an excellent decision you made. It is extremely easy for people to give themselves a hard time when a decision they made did not reach the fruition they hoped; however, it is important, when a decision does reach fruition, to appreciate you have done well.

The importance of learning to accept responsibility for your own life

I am aware many people have no idea how to accept responsibility for their own life. I have previously said a considerable amount which I hope you will be able to take on board; however, I would like to add a little more about the importance of this subject.

Every time a life is commenced there are two specific lessons each of you needs to learn, and they need to be learned throughout every lifetime. It is of the utmost importance each of you is aware of how to accept responsibility and develop self-love. (I will say a few more words in regard to self-love at a later point in this chapter.) It is vital you accept responsibility for your actions, and we feel this lesson needs to be learned time after time in the hope of ensuring there is no doubt in your mind who is responsible for you. There are those of you who have struggled with this concept in a great many lives and as a consequence it becomes something of an ordeal to be presented with this issue. We believe, here in spirit, that it is necessary for everybody to appreciate the importance of personal responsibility, hence this needs to be learned in every lifetime. We think it's important each of you are given a great many opportunities in which to learn personal responsibility; however, it seems for some even that is not enough. Some of you, even in old age, choose to blame everybody else for your own actions; it is curious there are so many who struggle with this. I cannot say enough how important it is that all of you focus your attention on learning this lesson, as ultimately nobody else is responsible for that. This is one aspect of your life that is entirely down to you, and I hope that with what I have yet to say you will be able to gain a greater understanding of the importance of personal responsibility.

How is that possible?

For the most part it is simply an understanding that you and only you are responsible for how you behave. If you are willing to behave in a particular way then it is necessary to understand the repercussions of your behaviour and to appreciate that whatever happens as a result is entirely down to you. If you are asked to behave in a way that does not sit well with you then it is important you either voice your concerns or remove yourself from the situation; however, if you do not and you continue to participate in that behaviour then the outcome of that event is down to you. I have covered this earlier in this chapter, but it is simply not possible for me to stress enough how important it is to understand the need to be responsible for your own behaviour. It is not our expectation that as soon as you reach a particular age you will become responsible for yourself, as we accept wholeheartedly that people mature at different rates and lives are considerably different; however, there is no excuse for anyone having reached adulthood to still be fobbing off the responsibility for their actions on anyone else. This is a strong indication that you are unable to accept a level of maturity, as this inability is something associated with children and that is to be expected, as their parents are, for the most part, responsible for how they behave. It is only as a child reaches maturity that they become able to understand that not everything their parents say is acceptable to them, and it then becomes necessary to consider all their parents have taught them and to appreciate that may not necessarily work for them either. It is important this process is undergone by all of you as it is simply unacceptable to behave in a way that has less-than-favourable repercussions and then blame your parents or anybody else, as that behaviour was in fact your own. Do you see? I hope you are able to appreciate the necessity of accepting responsibility for your behaviour, as in many instances the person who is being blamed is not in fact aware of what you are doing, and in instances like that how can they possibly be held responsible? All adults need to accept the responsibility for their own actions and not blame anybody else for what they do. I appreciate wholeheartedly for many that will be a difficult task to fulfil; however, if you only learn one thing in your life that you are able to take home with you it should be that.

The importance of self-love

This again is something that needs to be learned through every lifetime as it is necessary on your return home to be fully appreciative of the importance of caring for yourself. In many ways the concepts of self-love and personal responsibility overlap, and I think in order to be successful at either it is necessary to appreciate the importance of self-love.

Each of you is on earth to achieve a greater appreciation of not only how important you are and to learn to put yourself first, but also to accept and understand the needs of you and your body. Some of these are really quite basic, like ensuring a good quality of nutrition and exercise, and a level of comfort within your life. If a person feels unable to accept these basic requirements then it is often an indication of a lack of self-love, and this is something that needs to be addressed as you are all worthy of not only these basic requirements for life, but also a great deal of benefit and kindness that is available to you. It is important a standard of living is aspired to that offers a great deal of comfort and pleasure, as it was never our desire for any of you to endure a substandard quality of life. You may all be wondering at this point about those who struggle to find food to eat each day (and I am not referring to those who are homeless in the developed world). They are in fact learning the value of life and that is an entirely different lesson; however, we do not believe a person who is seeking to find food every day will be reading this book, as their priorities are considerably different to your own, and that is the reason this book has been pitched to those of you who have an adequate supply of food, water and shelter.

Many of you feel a lack of worth for the basic needs each of you require; however, that is something you need to learn as you are without doubt as worthy as everybody else on this planet to have these and it is important you are able to accept that. Simply because a person struggles with this concept, it does not give anybody else the right to try and force the need for self-love onto them as it is important this concept is learned by each of you. In fact, I am not at all sure it is even possible to force another person to have a greater opinion of themselves as that is something that comes from within and it needs to be a belief each of you is able to hold dear. For many it will take a considerable amount of hard work to understand the concept that you are worthy; however, that does not mean you are free to partake in gluttony or greed or to live in an enormous house all in the name of self-love, as that does in fact fall at the opposite end of the spectrum. To overindulge in any way is actually an indication of a lack of self-love, as for those who overindulge there is often insufficient self-love and as a result they feel the need to overdo their efforts to achieve it; however, it is important self-love is felt within and not provided from the outside. Do you see the point I am trying to make, that it is necessary for each of you to feel a great deal of self-love and to live your life in the knowledge that you are indeed a worthy individual? Individuals who choose to deny themselves basic comforts, or who choose to overdo this concept, indicate that they are lacking in self-love. It may of course be that you are in the enviable position of having a great deal of money and are able to live in a large and comfortable house; not all those who live in large houses lack self-love. The point I am trying to make is that people who think it is of the utmost importance to live in a large house simply because that is what they want often lack sufficient self-love. It is important all of you are able to feel this concept. I am hopeful I have made that point clear as I am aware parts of it are somewhat subtle.

How to appreciate your own importance

There are a number of ways to steadily grow in self-love and one of those is to offer yourself some time each day to do something you particularly enjoy. It may be you have a great love for sewing or reading or painting, in which case it would be excellent to partake in this exercise, as it offers you a level of pleasure. It may be you enjoy a particular sport, so if you were able to either participate in that sport or perhaps give yourself some time to watch it at some point during your week; again this reinforces a sense of your own importance. It may be you particularly enjoy the feelings that come with a beauty treatment or a visit to the barber, in which case this is something that would do you a great deal of good. It is essential to maintain these kindnesses to yourself throughout your life as in order to fully appreciate how important you are it is necessary to place your needs high on the list of things that need to be accomplished. It is also necessary to ensure other needs are met, for instance excellent nutrition, adequate sleep, fun in your life and enjoying the company of others. These are all things that need to be in your life, if not on a daily basis, then very close to that. They are basic needs each of you have, and if you choose to deprive yourself of them it reinforces the belief that you are not worthy, and that is simply not the case. I appreciate for those of you who struggle with this concept it will be extremely difficult to simply accept what I am saying and to put these measures in place; however, if that is what you choose to do it will, over time, convince you that you are indeed worthy. The reason some of you struggle with this is because it is something you have struggled with in previous lives, and in each subsequent life the challenge becomes harder in the hope that you are able to focus a greater amount of your energies on the importance of caring for yourself.

So you see, it is very much in your best interests to understand this concept and take it on board. There is nothing to be gained by martyring yourself and refusing to accept how important you are, as every one of you is as important as everybody else. There is not one person on this planet that has any less worth than anybody else, and it is vital you remember that and provide yourself with your basic needs.

It may be you are able to take on board some of these needs, which is an indication you are worth something; however, it is of the utmost importance you are able to embrace the full concept of self-love. There are no half measures with this one; it needs to be fully embraced. I think it is necessary for those of you who struggle with this concept to be aware of how tiring this can be for those around you, unless of course everybody around you is also struggling with this lesson. To be with someone who constantly martyrs themselves for the benefit of others is really rather unpleasant, and for those indulging in this type of behaviour I would like to advise you there is no benefit to it whatsoever and I cannot encourage you enough to stop it immediately. Even if to begin with you are only able to understand the concept rather than put it into action, that is a step in the right direction, and once you are able to do that I encourage you to perhaps put into action what I have suggested even though you may not necessarily feel that way. If you are able to do this, you will find your levels of self-love will start to increase, and that really is all there is to this one.

It is important to give yourself time and ensure your needs are met. I hope that is clear and you are able to understand this concept as it is something you will struggle with throughout your life if you are unable to grasp it, and you will continue to struggle with it both on your return home and throughout subsequent lives until you have a thorough understanding of how important each of you is. I cannot say this enough and I am struggling to end this as I have a need to continue repeating how important this is. So, I will stop now and leave this information with you in the hope you are able to allow it to permeate, and it will give you the incentive to increase your levels of self-love.

21 How to Make the Most of Your Time on Earth

This is a subject I have covered a number of times and I hope you all now have a good idea of the best way to live your life while you are on earth. However, there are a few things I would like to add and I am hopeful they will put into perspective much of what I have said up till now. I think it's important to have a good understanding of your reasons for being on earth, and they are of course to learn, grow and enjoy yourself. Two of the lessons you are there to learn are personal responsibility and self-love, and that is the case for everybody who incarnates on earth. It is the nature of the lessons themselves that varies from person to person and I would like to offer some information about how to achieve these lessons.

Each of you arrives on earth with a list of lessons you are hoping to learn. Your guides are there to offer you as many opportunities as possible to learn these lessons and it is hoped throughout your life on earth many of you will achieve your aims; however, there are those who seem determined to remain locked in a life full of fear and unable to step out of their comfort zone and achieve their aims. This is somewhat unfortunate as not only will you be disappointed on your return home but your guides will have worked extremely hard for remarkably little gain, and it is in those instances that people find how much disappointment and upset it is possible to achieve from a life on earth. I feel sure there are many of you reading this who are aware of the fears that rule your life and prevent you from having the life you intended to have; however, I rather suspect there are a number of others who are unaware of how much fear there is in their life. It is to those of you I would like to speak as I believe there are a great many of you who have somehow managed to believe that you are living a fulfilling life when in fact it is a life of fear. This limits a great deal of what you are able to achieve on earth as fear is something that prevents many of you from living a full life and becoming the person you hoped to become. This means some of you will spend many years on your return home feeling somewhat frustrated and disappointed at your lack of progress, and that the progress you had hoped to achieve while on earth is reflected in the level you are able to associate with in spirit. Eventually the frustration will build sufficiently that you choose to return to earth; however, this time it is likely the struggle will be even harder in the hope of forcing you to overcome those fears, and so again you are presented with a life full of fear that requires you to overcome it and develop into the person you hope to be. So you see, there is a constant cycle of frustration and disappointment that occurs in the lives of those who are shrouded in fear, and it is important to have a clear understanding of what will happen if you are unable to free yourself from it. Many of you are so well ensconced in your fears that you seem oblivious to how life could possibly be, and I am hopeful what I have to say will allow you to break free.

Those of you who struggle with fear will be aware of how limiting it can be, and it rather depends on how your fears manifest in your life. It may be leaving your home is a struggle, or it could be mixing with people that causes you something of a strain, or it may be that it is necessary for you to perform a series of tasks before you are able to even leave the house. There are all kinds of ways that fears can limit your self-expression and your ability to achieve your aims, and I feel sure the vast majority of you would dearly love to overcome your fears. Many of you are very aware of how limiting fear can be, even though I appreciate there is a level of safety in hanging on to your fears.

It is perhaps important to spend some time considering how your fears came about in the first place. It may well be they are a result of a particular incident, or they quietly developed over a number of years and somehow seemed to offer support, and perhaps became a way to continue with your life, as they helped you overcome a much greater fear. There are in fact a number of reasons why these fears may have developed and I would like to offer you a few suggestions to try and break them down. It is important, however, to tackle one fear at a time as to try and overcome all of them at once would simply be far too radical a change in your life, and my concern then would be that life would be so different and you would have so little grasp of who you truly are that, in order to try and recover, you might instead choose to regress to your former state, and so ultimately nothing is gained. I feel if you are able to tackle one fear at a time you will feel the change within you, and I am hopeful this will offer a great deal more confidence for focusing on other fears.

So, I would like you to select one particular fear – it matters not whether it is a large or a small fear – and sit quietly in the hope of understanding where this fear comes from. I would then like you to try and understand how this fear benefits your life. Consider what your life could be like if this fear was no longer in it, and how you could overcome it. It may be you simply need a particularly strong will in order to stop yourself repeating some form of behaviour; however, if you have reached a point where you are aware of the limiting effect of your fear then I think many of you will be able to put this into practice. It may help if you were to offer yourself a time frame in which to achieve this, and I would urge you to be generous with yourself. I have no great wish for you to anticipate this being achieved in a short period of time and then to struggle with disappointment on being unable to achieve your aim; it would be far better to offer yourself an extended period of time and then gradually over that period stretch yourself to try and overcome this fear in the hope you are able to steadily strengthen your resolve. It is important you are able to acknowledge your achievements as there was a good reason for you developing this fear; however, it has now become too limiting in your life to maintain. Please remember to be kind to yourself and to appreciate what you are achieving. My concern with this is you may have a period of struggle in trying to overcome your fear and then slip back into a pattern of behaviour that maintains it, and there is, as you well know, nothing to be gained by this, at least in the long term. It is important to be extremely brave in your desire to overcome this limiting fear. There is little fun and enjoyment for any of you if you then spend your time being particularly hard on yourself for any lack of progress, and so I would like to encourage you to find a way of congratulating yourself on any steps forward you are able to make. Try not to focus your attention on all the other fears you have yet to overcome; simply focus your mind on this particular one and you will find over time your ability to overcome it will steadily build, and I hope when you do indeed manage to overcome this fear you are able to celebrate in a way that offers you a great deal of encouragement for continuing to overcome more in the future.

It is important you are able to do this, as many, I feel sure, will be extremely hard on themselves, and where is the incentive to continue working to overcome your fears if all you are feeling as a result of it is hardship and unpleasantness? It may even be a good idea to begin this task by listing the fears you hope to overcome and then have some kind of preselected celebration for when you defeat each one, as this will offer an incentive to break free and overcome your fears. It is important to do this for yourself as it will allow you to have a far better life, and on your return home there will be a considerable celebration that you have managed to overcome your fears. It may be you have so many that they take many years to overcome; however, I urge you to remain focused and to continue working to overcome them as the gains are frankly enormous. You may choose throughout this period to have some professional help and I would like to encourage all of you, if that is your choice, to seek help from people who are specialised in overcoming fears, as this has the potential to offer you a great deal of support and encouragement. I am not sure it's possible to ever have enough encouragement and support while you are trying to overcome fears, and I am hopeful that with a great deal of determination you are able to achieve your aims.

Your life will change considerably as gradually you are able to see how much you have gained by freeing yourself from these limiting fears, and I am hopeful you are able to progress this development in your life as you take stock and appreciate the gains you are making. There is simply no need for any of you to be hard on yourself or to focus on your lack of progress. It is important you are able to continue with your aim of overcoming your fears despite any setbacks you believe you experience. It is, after all, a journey of learning, and while you may feel you are experiencing a setback there is always learning to be achieved within it; it is a matter of recognising and taking that learning on board in the hope that next time you choose to overcome this particular fear you are armed with a greater level of knowledge and understanding about why it is there in the first place, which will offer you greater levels of encouragement. There is so much to be gained by all of you if you are able to remain focused in overcoming your fears, and I cannot encourage you enough to remain true to those aims as the benefits you will gain are truly enormous; in fact, for some of you it is possible for your life to change completely.

How important it is to remain focused

I appreciate for many this will be particularly difficult as your fears developed for good reasons. It is unfortunate that, in order to cope with a particular situation, these fears developed in the first place; however, each of you can be particularly creative in finding ways to adjust to situations, and it may be that adopting a number of limiting fears enabled you to achieve something else. This fear, however, has over time become a much greater problem than the need to overcome the original event.

There are occasions when fear may in fact do you a great deal of good. If by overcoming your fears you find your life has far more risk within it, then I would question your desire to overcome those fears. If on the other hand your life has a great deal to gain by overcoming your fears then it is likely they are worth focusing on, and I am hopeful that is what each of you is able to do, as the benefits are truly magnificent. In your endeavours to overcome your fears it is necessary to remain focused as it may take a great deal of time; however, it is extremely important to do. Perhaps return to the list of fears you have a desire to overcome and reflect on that list regularly in order to remind yourself of your aims. I would like to encourage you to achieve something in the hope of stepping a little closer to overcoming at least one of those fears, and I say that as I have no wish for any of you to use your list as a reason to be hard on yourself due to a lack of progress. This list is only to be used to remain focused, as many of you have busy lives and there is a tendency to become so engrossed in coping with life that it's easy to forget the aims you were trying to achieve, and that is the only reason I suggest making a list.

So, you now have a list and you are encouraging yourself in ways that will invite you to remain true and steady, and also you have celebrations planned for when your fears are overcome. I would now like you to put in place a description for how you think you would benefit by overcoming these fears, and I would like you to be as descriptive as possible in the hope you have an extremely clear idea of what you can achieve. Be as expansive as you can in the hope you are fully focused on the potential you have. It would be particularly helpful if you were to itemise smaller steps that can be achieved along the way, as there is an excessive amount of expectation if you are only able to offer suggestions of how your life could possibly be with nothing along the way. Should it occur that you feel a lack of progress then it's easy to be hard on yourself, when in fact, in order to reach your final goal, there are a number of many smaller steps you would do well to achieve first. It is important to give that a considerable amount of time so you are clear in your mind about the smaller steps it is possible to reach before overcoming this fear completely. As you achieve each step, I would like you to be particularly kind and encouraging to yourself for making this progress, as to overcome a fear requires a great deal of courage because fears are put in place for what is perceived to be an excellent reason, even though those reasons no longer serve you and have become somewhat limiting.

How to be brave and step outside your comfort zone

It may be important to practise in order to be prepared for the day when you are able to stand firm and take a step towards overcoming your fear. If, for instance, it is difficult to stand up to a particular person, then perhaps practising in a mirror may be a good idea, or find a friend who is willing to help with a role play in the hope that when the situation does present itself you have already faced a number of possible outcomes and the event itself is not quite as horrifying as you imagined. Do you see how important it is to work to overcome your limiting fears? I feel sure you are able to adapt your preparations to whatever fear it is that is limiting your life. It may be you need to be particularly creative; however, there are without doubt ways to overcome your fear.

22

How to Have a Clear Understanding of the Need to Reach Your Potential

Many of you, on your return home to spirit, are disappointed that it was not possible to become the person you hoped to become, and I am hopeful this book will provide you with a much greater incentive as well as information on how that goal can be achieved. Each of you on your return home spends a great deal of time discussing what happened on earth, and there is often an overwhelming sadness because so many feel they were unable to develop themselves to the degree they had hoped. Once a person is aware of their intended date of arrival on earth there is a great deal of discussion in spirit about what they feel able to achieve, and people often get quite carried away with how much progress they believe they will be able to make. Then they arrive on earth and remember that actually it is not quite as easy as they thought, and many will return home full of disappointment and heartache that all their hopes and dreams came to remarkably little.

That is one reason for this book: to offer you information and guidance so that each of you is able to reach your full potential. We do have another reason for hoping you achieve this, and that is our desire for earth to become a much more pleasant place for everybody to live. We believe if more of you were able to embrace your potential and become the people you hoped to be then this would be a significant step in the right direction. We are aware many changes need to occur before this can happen, which we believe are occurring in your world and will continue to occur for the foreseeable future. We are hopeful that, with the information I provide in this book and a great many other occurrences spirit are planning, at some point in the not-too-distant future your world will become a significantly easier place for you all to live. It is very much our hope that each of you will be able to find a way to be kinder to yourself and each other, and if you are able to achieve this then the effects will spread throughout your world. It does not take so much change to occur to have a remarkable impact on a great many nations and the people within them; however, while I believe the ball has certainly started rolling, I would like it to gain a much greater momentum. This book is simply one way that it's possible for you all to embrace change, which is of course the reason I offered so much information on how to improve the quality of your lives and achieve what you intended to achieve. I appreciate for many of you that will seem something of a tall order; however, please do not underestimate the effects each of you can have on the world.

I fully appreciate for many there is a sense of futility when it comes to improving your world; however, all any of you can do is focus your energies on yourself, and we simply require sufficient people to do that to make magnificent changes. This progress has, in fact, been going on for many years now and is gathering significant momentum, and I hope with the information contained in this book we can further develop that momentum.

Many of you, I feel sure, will be thinking about the various areas of unrest in your world, and I have no wish to underestimate the impact that is having on people's lives. However, in order to achieve a significant improvement in many of your lives it is not necessary to have absolutely everybody on board; all it requires is a significant number. So you see, it is of the utmost importance that many more of you focus your attention on reaching your full potential in the hope of becoming a more well-rounded individual who is capable of showing great kindness and compassion to not only yourself, but others too. There is a great deal going on in your world with this in mind, and we are hopeful you will all be able to benefit from these changes.

How each of you can achieve your potential

If you are just beginning this journey of understanding and development it may well seem the journey you have yet to undertake is an extremely long one, but I would like to reassure you the only way to complete this journey is to begin it, and I am of the belief that, having reached this part of the book, you are now on a very significant journey, and that pleases me more than you could ever imagine. I am hopeful that in the fullness of time you will feel able to continue your journey as, while the beginning may be something of a trial and likely feel rather overwhelming with all you need to overcome, there is also a sense of being on a journey that will significantly alter your life, and very much for the better. From our observations of people over a great many years, it is remarkable how many of them change significantly, and in a very short while their lives become considerably easier. The important part of this journey is beginning it, and I feel that is what each and every one of you reading this has done. I cannot overestimate the benefits you will feel in your life if you are able to adopt many of the strategies and suggestions I have given throughout this book, and I hope that is exactly what you choose to do.

How to begin this journey

Many of you may feel somewhat overwhelmed by how much there is in your life that needs to change, and I would like to make a few suggestions about how to begin. It is important each of you has a list to help guide you forward, and look back and appreciate how much you have achieved. Make sure this list has a date, in order to get from it what you hope. Once you have commenced your list it is necessary to spend some time considering how big or small your aims are, and it is important to break this down into stages in the hope you are able to take smaller steps towards your main aim. I have no wish for any of you to leap in and try to achieve the biggest aim you have without first considering smaller steps in the hope of making it easier to reach the final outcome. The danger is that if you step straight in and try to change your whole life then there is a high probability you will simply lose your footing and choose to abandon this project. It is necessary each of you is fully able to appreciate the importance of the work you are doing, and to allow yourself the necessary steps that need to be taken before you are better equipped to deal with the larger issue. This also means that, by taking a number of smaller steps, the main challenge will be considerably smaller when you do finally reach it, and that is something each of you needs to consider. There is nothing to be gained by attempting to achieve everything and then struggling with a lack of success, or even giving yourself such a hard time you choose not to attempt such development again. It is important you are aware of the bigger picture, which is to reach your full potential, and to do that in significantly smaller steps. If you are able to do this the likelihood of success is notably greater, and I cannot wish that enough for you.

23 How to Progress in This Life

I say again, many of you will feel I have covered this a number of times; however, there is more I would like to add and I believe it is of the utmost importance in ensuring your needs are met, and I say that from a spiritual point of view.

I have previously covered the need for each of you to become aware of the reason you are on earth, which for the most part is to learn, grow and have a great deal of fun, and in order to make the most of that it is important to be particularly courageous and overcome a great deal of negativity in many different forms. There is, however, one area I have yet to cover and I am hopeful you will find this particularly helpful, and that is how to receive a great deal of help.

I am aware many of you will read this book and feel a little overwhelmed with the amount of progress you may feel you have yet to attain; however, I would like to advise you that there is in fact a great deal of help out there for you and all you have to do is ask. It may be you require a level of sensitivity to appreciate the help that is offered; however, if you are not a particularly sensitive person I am hopeful it will have been possible for you to make lists of what you are hoping to achieve, and having requested help you may well become aware of an increased speed in achieving your aims.

What is the help I am suggesting you request?

There are a number of other energetic beings who are on this earth as it is not, in fact, only spirit that walks with you; however, for the vast majority it is simply not possible to be aware of these beings. They come in peace and for the most part their aim is to help those who are currently walking the earth. They do this because, like many of us in spirit, they believe the journeys each of you have on earth are particularly arduous and it is their desire to try and lift that journey. They hope by offering their help to lighten your load, they will make your time on earth somewhat easier. It may be you find yourself stuck in a particularly difficult situation and put out a request for help, and while they will do all they possibly can to ease the situation you find yourself in, it may be your expectation of what you would like them to do is simply not possible, so there may be a sense that they are unwilling to aid you in your struggle; however, that is not necessarily the case. It may well be a number of beings have worked particularly hard to try and ease the struggle you are enduring; however, if your expectation is for them to remove the struggle from your life then that may not be possible as it may be something that is important for you to learn and grow from, so there would be no benefit if they were to take that struggle away. All they can do is offer some support and guidance in how to learn from it a little more easily.

So you see, it's important to be open to any help that is offered. The important point of this is that it's necessary to ask for that help. Help will never be given unless it is requested as we do not believe we should offer our help unless you feel it is needed, and so the responsibility is very much with you to ask for help if you would like it. It may be the situation you find yourself in is bobbing along really rather nicely and you do not feel there is much to be gained by asking for help; however, that is not always the case and it is likely there are many who will find themselves struggling a great deal and would very much appreciate some help, in which case all you have to do is ask. It may be the help that is offered is not quite how you hoped it would be; however, it is up to you whether you choose to accept that help or not. It may be you feel the cost of the help is not something you wish to accept, as energetic beings will work particularly hard to offer any help they can; however, there are occasions when there are downsides to that as it may simply not be possible for them to provide you with help without some kind of price being paid. That is not necessarily how we would like it to be; however, there are occasions when it is simply not possible to offer the help you would like without some kind of consequence to you. We work hard to try and not make this the case but sometimes it is simply unavoidable. We would also like to say we appreciate that for some of you there is an element of wanting to have a great deal, and that is not what asking for help is all about. It is about making the situation you find yourself in somewhat easier, rather than giving you all the material goods you think you need. Having said that, we appreciate there are occasions when it is necessary to have a material item and in those instances we will do our best to provide you with that item in some form; however, please understand that it's not always possible for us to achieve that, although we will do our best.

There is one other point I would like to advise you of, and that is that each of these beings requires time in order to be able to effect the changes you hope for. Generally, it is impossible to fulfil a request immediately, as often a great deal of planning needs to be achieved before it is possible for you to be aware of any changes, and it is important all of you are aware of this.

Ways it may benefit you if you were to ask for help

I am aware there are many of you who would like help with pretty much everything, but there is not so much to be gained from that. So, my suggestion is to perhaps request help in situations where you are struggling, as it can become somewhat tiresome for us if people are constantly requesting help with every little thing in their lives, as you are there to live your life and to learn and grow from it, so it is important you allow yourself that opportunity. There are, however, without doubt times in all your lives when the struggles become a little overwhelming and these are excellent opportunities to request some help. We will do our best to fulfil that desire. It may be there is a particular direction you would like your life to go in; however, there are occasions when people have a desire to progress in a direction that is not in fact to their benefit, and while we have no great wish for you to be disappointed there is no inclination on our part to develop your progress in a direction that does not benefit you. So, we might offer a number of stumbling blocks for you to trip over in the hope you will appreciate this is not a direction that benefits you. We are hopeful each of you will be aware that if a journey appears to be particularly difficult it may simply be because this is not a journey that has so much benefit for your life. It may also be we are working hard to try and bring your life back on track and head in the direction you originally hoped it would.

Many of you find yourselves pursuing a completely different avenue of progress to what you initially hoped for, and while your life may feel successful it becomes necessary for us to bring you back to a place where you are able to achieve the aims you are on earth to achieve. We are in many ways your servants in offering you the opportunities to achieve what you set out to achieve. There are people amongst you who feel absolutely determined to follow a particular avenue, and while this is not an avenue that has any great benefit it nonetheless works well for you at that particular time, so we have no great desire to change your current path, and it may, in fact, be a while before we take steps to try and bring you back to your intended path.

There are also those amongst you who made a decision before you incarnated about a particular aspect of your life which you later choose to change; for instance, you may have chosen not to have children or perhaps to only have one child, and after a number of years on earth you have a desire to change that wish. We will do our best to keep you on track to your original aim; however, if this desire becomes overwhelming on your part we will work to try and update your needs and perhaps put in place opportunities to achieve your new aim, as we appreciate there are times when a person's desires change.

We do find the question of children somewhat difficult, as in previous lives many of you were overwhelmed with the number of children you had and decisions were made before you incarnated not to have any or to have perhaps one or two. However, that need may change while you are on earth due to a number of reasons and so it is up to us to consider your new needs and to make a decision about whether or not it is to your benefit to let this happen. While you may well feel rather uncomfortable that we are the ones who allow that decision to progress or not, I would like to remind you we are also the ones who are fully aware of what will happen in your life, and it may be that while something seems a particularly good idea in the present it is not in fact such a great idea a number of years down the line. Do you see? I hope it is clear that we will always offer help if we possibly can. There are occasions when consequences are attached to that; however, that is simply because we are unable to arrange help any other way, and while it may feel rather uncomfortable to be aware of the decisions we are making on your behalf, I would like to remind you we are more aware of the aims of your life than you currently are.

How to change the direction of your life

It may well be you are trotting along quite nicely with your life and suddenly it appears your life is about to veer off at something of a tangent. If you have been happy with your life up till this point it can come as something of a shock. It may be this is not something we planned; it may simply be a consequence of something else, in which case I would like to request each of you spends some time sitting quietly with yourself to understand how you feel in regard to how this adventure may pan out. It is important to have a sense of your reaction to this opportunity, and I am hopeful that when you do, especially given the information I have already provided in this book, it will become somewhat easier to appreciate whether or not this is an ideal opportunity to pursue. It may also be that this new opportunity is something you would do well to avoid and so it's important to give yourself that time to understand how you feel. Do you see? Not everything offered has your benefit in mind; it may be a new opportunity that is offered is in fact highly beneficial to someone else and will not benefit you at all, so it is necessary to give yourself some time to consider the change in direction in the hope of either remaining where you are or taking up a new opportunity that will benefit you a great deal.

I appreciate wholeheartedly that this can be particularly difficult to grasp as not all of you are sensitive to the feelings within your body, and it then requires a great deal of brain work to consider whether or not a particular opportunity has any benefit to you. If you choose to take this new opportunity and it does not benefit your life we will do our best to guide you back in the hope you are able to get the most from your life.

24

How to Make the Most of Your Skills

I am hopeful each of you has a clear understanding of the kinds of things it's important to focus your attention on; however, there are a few items I would like to ensure you are completely clear on. I have spoken of them before, and I would now like to expand a little on them. Firstly, I think it's important more attention is given to the subject of how you can all do more to reach your potential. I have offered a number of ideas about how that's possible and I am hopeful with a little more information you will all be able to achieve exactly that. So, it is very much my hope each of you will feel able to give more of your attention to this subject, as I believe there is a great deal to be gained by reaching your potential. Some of you manage it, but a great many currently do not and it is those I wish to aim this information at, as there is much to be gained.

Each of you arrive on earth with a clear idea of what you hope to achieve while you are there; however, less clear before you incarnate are the kinds of difficulties you are likely to face given the skills you arrive there with, and it is these skills I would like to elaborate on. It is important when you incarnate that you are offered the skills you held when you left your last incarnation in the hope of being able to develop them further. It may be your last life was particularly hard or remarkably easy, but that makes no difference to the skills you are provided with as these refer to your mental ability to deal with your life. Given any kind of situation, each of you will respond in a different way and the way you respond may be only slightly different to anybody else; however, it will always be different. The reason for that is because of the skills you have brought forward from your previous life, and it is these I am hoping to offer some information about as I think there is a great deal each of you is able to do to further these skills. I do not necessarily mean skills in the traditional sense of talents you are able to use, perhaps in the workplace or for your enjoyment; I mean in the sense of how you are able to respond to a situation in a particular way. Each of you has a set of criteria built into you which ensure you respond in a similar way to how you would have done in your previous life. It is, however, possible in this life to learn and grow and therefore develop different skills in order to respond in a different way the next time a particular situation presents itself, and it is hoped that throughout your lives these skills will steadily develop so that during your last life on earth you are able to steer your way through most situations with a degree of skill and understanding for what is truly going on.

How to further develop these skills

For the most part developing these skills is part of your learning throughout your life; however, it is possible to work a little harder in the hope of improving, and the best way to do that is to try and get an understanding of the reasons you struggle in particular situations. It may be that you struggle to offer suggestions, or it may be you struggle to understand the reason people do not pay attention to what you have to say, or you find listening to the ideas of others rather a challenge; and so I think it's important to try and focus your attention on why you believe that to be the case. Many of you will very likely try to pin this on events that occurred in your childhood, and for some that may indeed be the case; however, there are others who have brought through particular behaviours from a number of previous lives. It is generally something they have tried many times to understand, although it can also be just from the previous life, and I would like to suggest a technique which I think many of you could benefit from.

When you are presented with a scenario that has been presented to you a number of times before (as these types of situations most certainly will have been, and we have discussed this in terms of learning what you intended to learn;) however, this particular one is a little different. I would like it very much if you felt able to spend some time focusing on what it is that stops you being able to consider others in these types of situations. It may be you are feeling so uncomfortable that you forget the importance of others' opinions, or that you feel your opinion is far superior to other people's, which of course is an illusion. It is important time is given to this in order to get a full grasp of what is preventing you from developing this level of understanding. When you have done that, it is then important to do your best the next time a particular situation presents itself to ensure a different response. Ideally it would be best to not only offer a different response, but to be very aware of your actions in that particular scenario. I appreciate that is not always easy; however, given that you are now wiser to what is going on I am hoping it will be possible to alert yourself to a particular situation that is being presented. It may of course be that it's simply not possible to respond differently the next time a particular situation is presented; however, it may be possible the time after that, or the time after that. It is not something that will go away until an alteration in your behaviour is achieved.

This particular scenario is a little different to learning your lessons as for the most part learning lessons is simply an understanding of what is going on, whereas this requires a level of understanding and also a response, and it is not quite so necessary when learning lessons to provide a response, though it may be. During your learning it might be necessary to begin responding in different ways; however, it is never acceptable while developing your skills to simply have an understanding – it is necessary to respond in ways that are unfamiliar to you, at least initially. It is during this learning that you are able to develop your skills, and these skills are very important in how well you work with other people. I am aware that the difference between the two is somewhat subtle; however, I hope you are able to observe the difference, as being able to develop these skills enables you to get on with other people considerably easier, and eases your journey on earth. It is important to be well developed in this regard. It may of course be that the people you are trying to work with have insufficient skills of their own, and so regardless of the skills you have developed they are unable to recognise your progress, in which case it will feel very much as if you are banging your head on a brick wall and there will be little to be gained, which makes the acknowledgement of your skills somewhat harder. It is, however, important to be as objective as possible. This can be difficult at times as it's easy to be in a significant amount of denial in regard to your own lack of development, and so you need to be as honest as you can with yourself. It is simply no good to either you or anybody else to ignore your lack of development or to continually make excuses for it, as ultimately you are the one who will pay the price; you are the one who will need to keep returning to earth in order to progress these skills. Do you see? It is all very well to blame other people for their lack of development, but if you feel it is likely to be you that is at fault it is important to address that as you are the one who will pay the price.

How to be open with yourself

I appreciate there are a number of you who will struggle considerably with what I have just said as I think many will be oblivious to the lack of development of their own skills. For some of you I believe there is an expectation that if you have reached a particular level in, for instance, your workplace, it is necessary to be the one with all the answers, and that of course is simply not the case as no one on this planet has the answer for everything. It is important to acknowledge that, and to try and appreciate that others may well have ideas better than your own, and I hope it will be possible for you to appreciate that it is not necessary to know the answers to everything.

It is equally important to have an understanding that simply because you have reached a particular level in your workplace it does not mean you are in charge of the lives of everybody who works for you. It is essential to appreciate you have reached that level because of your experience; however, many others have a great deal of experience also, and it is important to acknowledge that, and to not be afraid that their knowledge may be superior to your own, as you were selected to do your job due to other skills in your possession. I hope I am making this point clear as I would like all of you who are in positions of authority to appreciate that other people have a great many skills that need to be considered in order for you to make the most of the situation you find yourself in. There is little to be gained by ignoring that fact and working to prove your perfection for the job, as all that will do is cause a great deal of disharmony and upset and much of your time will be spent trying to control the behaviour of others, which is a waste of everybody's time. It is far better to consider your own skills and those of others, and to work together to develop the best result. I have tended to offer examples as they relate to the workplace; however, this approach works equally well in many other situations. I hope I have been able to make that clear to you.

Why it's necessary to grasp the importance of other people in your life

No man is an island, and no woman either, for that matter. Not one of you is on earth to live completely alone without any kind of stimulus from other people, and all those people who choose to have lives where they are isolated are kidding themselves if they think they are doing it for their own good, as there is nothing to be gained by living an isolated life. It is important to mix with people with the intention of developing your skills, learning your lessons, growing and of course having fun, and this is simply not possible if you live in a place where you cannot mix with other people. It is of the utmost importance for all of you to make a point of regularly being in situations where there are a number of people, and I am hopeful I am able to offer some information that will make this rather more desirable for you. Those of you who prefer your own company are less dependent on interaction with others, and while in one respect it is excellent you are able to develop your own judgement and rely on it, it is nonetheless necessary to have a great many more connections with other people, because otherwise there is no possibility of learning and growing.

The importance of making the most of these situations

It is all very well spending your time mixing with other people; however, it is important to make a great many attempts at improving the relationships you have with them, and I have given you a number of suggestions to achieve that. However, it is additionally important to appreciate that nobody on this planet is exactly like you, and you all need to make that adjustment when dealing with other people. It is all very well being aware of this, but it is necessary to make an allowance for it when you deal with others. There is little to be gained by making that allowance and then enforcing your own thoughts and opinions on those around you, as not only will this make you unpopular, it will also reduce what you manage to learn; and indeed one of the things you are there to learn may be to appreciate the opinions of others. You do not necessarily have to accept their opinions, but it is important to hear what they have to say and consider whether their ideas are in fact better than your own, and to be as objective about that as you can. There are many people out there who have far better ideas than you, and it is necessary to acknowledge that and even make the most of it.

How important it is to appreciate differences

This world would be a very different place if each of you thought and felt the same way, but in reality how dull would that be, with everything exactly the same? It would mean no acknowledgement of the uniqueness of you, or appreciation of that. It would, I feel sure, appear as though you were all automata incapable of individual thought, and that is, in fact, what makes your world rich and exciting. It is the differences that make your world such a truly unique place to be, and that is something worth celebrating rather than constantly struggling against. I really hope that's clear as I think many of you have so much to gain by embracing that fact, and I hope from here on in that is something all of you choose to do.

Conclusion

The importance of living a spiritual life

I have now covered all the aspects needed in order to encapsulate the points many of you need to examine, to help ease the strains and struggles within your lives. I am hopeful what I am about to offer will provide you with information about how to live a more spiritual life.

It is important, I believe, for each of you to have a much greater understanding of the struggles of other people. It is remarkably easy to go through life being aware that others are perhaps not coping quite as well as you are, and many I believe will offer a level of judgement in those cases. This may be done in the hope of improving your own life, or it may be because that is what all those around you choose to do, or there may be any number of other reasons you choose to have a less-than-supportive attitude to somebody in your life. It is extremely important all of you are aware that those around you are there to achieve their own lessons, which are being provided by their guides. It may be the lessons they hope to learn are very different to your own, or it may be their guides have chosen a different approach to how they learn what they need to learn, and it is important all of you are aware of that as no two of you will have exactly the same life. It may appear for a short while that your life is similar to someone else's, but that will never be the case throughout an entire life, and it is likely people you are particularly close to at one point will become rather distant in another part of your life. It is simply the way it is and no judgement is ever offered to anybody who is unable to maintain friendships throughout their life, though we appreciate many of you do manage that.

I would like to make a point that some of you may find rather enlightening, and that is that we work especially hard to ensure that when you are going through a particularly trying phase in your life, you have people around you who are there to try and support you. It may be these people are not the ones you hoped to have with you; however, they are there and it is our hope you will be able to use their friendship in order to help you through a particularly difficult period. It may of course be that the challenge requires you to cope very much alone, in which case there may only be a few people around (or none at all) to support you and there are indeed occasions when it's important to face situations alone in order to learn what you are there to learn.

We appreciate it is extremely difficult to understand what you are on earth to learn and grow from; however, all we ask is for you to have faith and understanding that what is happening to you is very much for your own good – unless of course there is an element of abuse or criminality, or any other negative form of behaviour. It is important each of you is aware that the lessons you are there to learn are of a positive nature and are opportunities to learn and grow from. It is never acceptable for any of you to bully or abuse another individual in any way, ever. However, if a person is learning to stand up for themselves and the relationship they are learning it in becomes abusive or bullying then it is important to remove yourself from that situation, as the learning part of that relationship has become negative and that is not the purpose of lesson learning.

I would also like to say something about how important it is to offer support and kindness to those around you. Many people are aware of the difficulties in their own life and tend to forget others are also struggling, and it may well be that simply by offering your kindness to another person you will ease the struggles within your own life. We appreciate that is not always easy to be aware of; however, it is something you would do well to consider, as the lives of many others would improve with kindness and help from yourself, and there may also be a significant improvement in your own life if you are able to do this. Still, it is important when assistance is offered to another person it is done from the kindness within you and not with the intention of improving your own life. Do you see? I hope that is clear as it is an important differentiation to understand, though I appreciate for many of you there is no need for me to even mention that point.

How important it is to have a greater respect for the animals that share your planet

I am aware that currently there is a great deal of abuse going on within your farming industry. The welfare of many of the animals reared within it is less than satisfactory and it is important greater respect is offered to these animals. It is not acceptable to eat their carcasses simply because they are a cheap form of food. I would like you to consider that, as these animals have had their lives shortened significantly so you can live in a way that you feel benefits you. There is, in fact, no need for any of you to eat the carcass of an animal, and there is without doubt plenty of other food available. I appreciate there are many arguments against this; however, each of you is in fact an animal and there are some rather cannibalistic tendencies amongst you that lead you to eat members of your own family. I know there are many who will struggle to understand this part of the book; however, it is important to make the point that, as no one would eat their immediate family, why would you eat your extended family? And by that, I mean the animals within your world. Many of these animals are kept in appalling conditions and slaughtered in even more appalling conditions, and many of us are horrified by the lack of respect given to these wondrous beings who lose their lives simply so you can have a meal that tastes a particular way. I am aware it is likely this portion of the book will provoke controversy; however, it is vital far less dependency for your food is placed on the lives of the animals that inhabit earth. They have as much right as every person to have respect. I will not say so much more on this subject; however, I hope you will all consider how important it is to have respect and understanding for all life on this planet, not simply that of humans.

In conclusion

I think many of you need to not only consider the importance of your own life, but to have a greater understanding of the kinds of lives other people live while they are on earth. Many of you have extremely difficult lives and this is because you simply have so much to learn. Those who are beginning your journey of enlightenment often struggle a great deal; however, those who have learned a considerable number of lessons tend to have lives that are somewhat easier. It is unfortunate it needs to be that way, but it is something each of you has agreed upon before you incarnated on earth. I am hopeful that, having read this book, you will have a greater understanding of not only your struggles, but those of other people; and, armed with this knowledge, a greater appreciation for the lives of others. I also hope this will provide you with greater tolerance and an ability to be more encouraging to others in the lives they lead. It is important to have a greater understanding of the struggles many endure while on earth, and it is of course necessary you are all able to appreciate that this is very much your choice.

I would also like to say something about the importance of accepting that you all have a choice. It is all very well knowing the information I have provided and being willing to continue your struggle; however, you do in fact all have a choice and it may be that at a particular time you simply do not feel able to participate in the learning that is offered, and we understand that. That is often the reason your lives are the length they are, in order to give you opportunities to learn and grow. You may be wondering why many people pass so young, and often this is because that is their choice. They were aware their struggle on earth would be considerable and they wished to be taken back home having only had a brief opportunity. They had no great wish to be involved in the struggles that many need to endure, so they incarnate, learn what they can as quickly as they can, and return home. There are others who knew their lives would be extremely difficult and they were offered an opportunity to return home and it was, in fact, their choice to either continue their struggle or opt out. Not all of you are given this opportunity, although a few are.

It is hoped by us, and you before you incarnate, that this opportunity will not in fact be used, but there are occasions when it is taken advantage of. This is somewhat unfortunate as it is often an indication that what you intended to learn has not in fact been learned, and proved to be simply too difficult to take on board. This means that the next time you have such an opportunity it will be harder to learn. So you see it is always easier to do your best to continue in your aim of learning and growing, as your life will be somewhat easier next time around when you return to earth with whatever lessons you choose to learn.

I am aware some of you would dearly like to opt out of your life, and I am hopeful that is a choice you do not make as there is always disappointment on your return home that it was not possible to complete your aims. It is often many years before there is another opportunity to return and try again, and of course then the lesson you are trying to learn will be somewhat harder; however, that is your choice. Many of you struggle a great deal in this life, and I hope with the information offered in this book you have a greater understanding of why that is the case. I also hope it will offer you some indications of how it's possible to take yourself out of that place of struggle. There really is no need for your entire life to be this way, and I hope the information offered here will help to lift you out of that place. It may of course make things a little worse for a while, but you will at least be furnished with information and knowledge that offer you an opportunity to elevate yourself out of the turmoil you are currently facing.

I also think it is important that many of you sit down and consider what you wish to achieve in this life. I appreciate that what you wish to achieve while you are on earth is likely to be somewhat different to what you wished to achieve while you were in spirit; however, if you do your best to step forward and achieve your aims from a human perspective it is likely that will make your journey somewhat lighter, and it will then be up to your guides to work around these aims to give you opportunities to learn and grow. So you see, it is very much up to you how you choose to live your life on earth.

I think it is essential all of you have an understanding of the importance of your time on earth and are willing to do your best to ensure not only that your aims are met, but that a great deal of fun is had, and when I say fun I mean things that give you pleasure; provided of course there is no detrimental effect to anyone or anything else. It is important this is embraced as it will make this life so much easier.

How to make the most of your future

I have said much about how to make the most of your life, and now it is over to you to put into practice all you feel is needed. We in spirit watch you all struggling and I am hopeful all that has been offered to you will make your life easier.

There is one last thing I would like to say, and that is how important it is for you all to be aware that none of you is ever alone. We are always with you, doing our best to encourage you to achieve all you have advised us you want to achieve, and we work hard to do that for you. Please remember this life is an adventure for you to enjoy, and we will do our best to ensure that is indeed what happens.

So, I would like to wish you all the very best of luck, and I hope and pray you are all able to find the courage and strength to achieve everything you hoped to achieve.